Lou Gehrig

Read all of the books in this exciting,
action-packed biography series!

Barry Bonds

Ichiro Suzuki

Lou Gehrig

Michelle Kwan

Mickey Mantle

Tim Duncan

SPORTS HEROES AND LEGENDS™

Lou Gehrig

by Kevin Viola

LERNER
SPORTS
AN IMPRINT OF LERNER PUBLISHING GROUP

For Matty V, Gelby, Scotty, Ogre, Menachem,
and Uncle Douglas. True fans, all.

LernerSports
An imprint of Lerner Publishing Group
241 First Avenue North
Minneapolis, MN 55401 U.S.A.

Website address: www.lernerbooks.com

Cover photograph:
Courtesy National Baseball Hall of Fame, Cooperstown, New York

Library of Congress Cataloging-in-Publication Data

Viola, Kevin, 1974–
    Lou Gehrig / by Kevin Viola.
        p.   cm. — (Sports heroes and legends)
    Includes bibliographical references and index.
        Contents: Prologue: The luckiest man—Little Lou—Another Babe?—Lou
    Lewis—Earning his stripes—The greatest team of all time—Lou and Babe—
    Ups and downs—Love and marriage—Captain Lou—A new partner—The
    streak and the slump—Epilogue: The pride of the Yankees.
        ISBN: 0–8225–1794–9 (lib. bdg. : alk. paper)
        1. Gehrig, Lou, 1903–1941—Juvenile literature. 2. Baseball players—
    United States—Biography—Juvenile literature. 3. New York Yankees
    (Baseball team)—Juvenile literature. [1. Gehrig, Lou, 1903–1941. 2. Baseball
    players. 3. New York Yankees (Baseball team)] I. Title. II. Series.
    GV865.G4V56 2005
    796.357'092—dc22   2003023649

Manufactured in the United States of America
1 2 3 4 5 6 – JR – 10 09 08 07 06 05

Contents

The Luckiest Man

On July 4, 1939, more than sixty-two thousand fans packed Yankee Stadium in New York City, talking excitedly about the show they were about to see. But no one was discussing the doubleheader between the Yanks and the Washington Senators that was to take place that day. They were talking about saying good-bye to a legendary Yankee player, the captain of the team—Lou Gehrig.

It was Lou Gehrig Appreciation Day. Everyone in the stadium knew that between the two games, a ceremony would mark the retirement of the veteran first baseman, but not everyone knew the awful truth. The truth was that Lou Gehrig—who was only thirty-six years old and who had been at the top of his game just two years ago—was dying.

Lou had been diagnosed with amyotrophic lateral sclerosis (ALS) only two weeks before. Ever since the last months of the

1938 season, he had been slowing down. His hitting wasn't as powerful, his baserunning wasn't as fast, and his fielding wasn't as accurate. Fans, sportswriters, and other players thought Lou had passed his prime. Thirty-six was old for a ballplayer, after all. Lou didn't want to believe that he was getting too old for the game, but even he couldn't figure out what was wrong with his body. Maybe everybody was right. Maybe his muscles and bones were just getting too old for baseball.

Then came the diagnosis that nobody had predicted. Lou had a deadly disease.

ALS weakens the muscles in the arms, hands, and legs. It causes twitching and cramping of muscles in the feet and hands and often makes the use of arms and legs more difficult. For example, it can cause a person who is simply walking down the street to lose his or her balance and stumble for no apparent reason. A person who has always been strong might suddenly have a hard time picking up something—like a pencil or a teacup—that was once simple to lift.

Lou Gehrig had been affected by all these symptoms, but until June 19, 1939, when the doctors told him he had ALS, he had no idea what was causing them. At first it was a relief to know that there was a reason for all his problems, but then the doctors told him he would never play baseball again. Lou wasn't surprised— for the last few months it had been almost impossible for him to hit the ball and run the bases. But the news still broke his heart. Playing baseball was Lou's favorite thing in the world, and it wasn't easy for him to admit that it was time to hang up his spikes.

So on that day in July, he came to say good-bye to his team, his fans, and the sport that had made him a star.

Most of the people in the stands on July 4 didn't know that Lou was dying. Lou himself hadn't been told that the disease was going to take his life. But he knew he was leaving behind the life he loved—the life of a professional baseball player. As he walked into the stadium that day, he was full of emotion.

After the first game between the Yankees and the Senators was over, Joe McCarthy, the Yankees manager, addressed the crowd. He was joined on the field by the current Yankees team, including Joe DiMaggio, as well as former teammates of Lou's. Even Babe Ruth showed up, although he and his former friend and teammate Lou hadn't spoken since 1934. The mayor of New York, Fiorello La Guardia, stood on the field to honor Lou. Lou's mother, father, and wife, Eleanor, all sat in the stands.

McCarthy made a short speech about what a great player and a fine man Lou was. Then a sportswriter named Sid Mercer took over the microphone and presented Lou with gifts from the players, from sportswriters, and from the Yankee organization itself. Even the New York Giants—the Yankees' rival team—had sent a farewell present for Lou.

Always a shy and quiet man, Lou was moved to tears by the outpouring of affection and at first didn't think he would be able to speak to the crowd. He whispered something in Mercer's ear, and Mercer repeated it into the microphone. "Lou has asked me to thank all of you. He is too moved to speak," Mercer said.

The crowd, however, wouldn't have it. They wanted to hear from their hero, and they began to chant, "We want Gehrig! We want Gehrig!"

What followed was one of the most famous speeches in the history of sports. *Sports Illustrated* writer Ron Fimrite wrote of Gehrig's speech: "The words are nearly as familiar to Americans, with even the remotest sense of history, as 'four score and seven years ago.'"

Lou tried to hold back his tears. He wiped at his face with his handkerchief and stepped forward. He was weak, and it clearly took effort for him to make the simple walk to the microphone. Once there, he tipped his head humbly and placed his hands on his hips. Surrounded by the Yankee stars of the past and the present—the men he'd traveled and worked and played with—Lou was overwhelmed by emotion. He had written his feelings down the night before, but when he began to speak, he had no notes. He spoke directly from the heart.

"Fans, for the past two weeks you have been reading about a bad break I got. Yet today I consider myself the luckiest man on the face of this earth." He went on to talk about how much he appreciated his fans, his teammates, his coaches, and his family. "I may have had a tough break," he concluded, "but I have an awful lot to live for."

Lou knew that even though his life was being cut short, he had been blessed to achieve so many things other men only dream of. He got to play professional baseball. He got to play for one of the greatest teams of all time. He was a superstar. He had traveled the country and the world, and he had friends, a wife, and parents who loved him.

As Lou finished his speech, the crowd went wild. Babe Ruth walked forward, hugged Lou, and whispered something in his ear—the first time the two had spoken in five years. Lou embraced his old friend, then turned and walked off the field for the last time. His number 4 jersey was retired permanently—the first-ever Yankees number to receive that honor. On that day, the fans, players, sportswriters, and members of the Yankee organization displayed their love for Lou in a way that he would never forget. It was a fitting good-bye for a man who had in many ways, for many years, been the heart of the New York Yankees.

Chapter | One

Little Lou

Heinrich Ludwig Gehrig, later to be known as Lou, was born on June 19, 1903, in the Yorkville section of New York City. It was a run-down neighborhood where many impoverished German and Hungarian immigrants lived. His parents, Christina and Heinrich Gehrig, were two of these immigrants. They had both moved to the United States from Germany in the late nineteenth century and had met and married in New York. They were both tall, stocky, and strong, so it was no surprise that little Heinrich weighed in at a whopping fourteen pounds—a real heavyweight of a newborn. His parents were happy that he seemed to be such a strong boy from the outset. They had already lost their firstborn son, who died when he was just a baby. They didn't want to lose another.

Happily, Heinrich did survive and would come to be called by the English version of his name, Henry Louis, nicknamed Lou so as not to be confused with his father. Christina would give birth to two more children: Sophie, who was born in 1904 and died of diphtheria when she was just under two years old, and Anna, who also passed away when she was an infant. Lou was the only child of four to survive.

The Gehrigs were not a wealthy family. Both of Lou's parents worked. His father was a metal leaf hammerer—a skilled metal craftsman who hammered designs into sheet metal to be used as decorations on furniture, stoves, and such. It was a high-paying job when there was work to be had, but Heinrich (or Henry) was often sick, which made it harder for him to land steady employment. He ended up spending much of his time in local bars and German gyms, complaining with his friends about the lack of work in New York and basically goofing off.

When Lou was a boy, his family never had money for an overcoat or a jacket for him, so he often walked around even on cold winter days in nothing but a shirt and light pants. Later in life, when Lou was a wealthy player for the Yankees, he still never wore a coat. He said he couldn't get used to the feel of them.

Meanwhile Lou's mother, Christina, hired herself out as a cook and a maid to wealthy families on the opposite side of town. She was an excellent chef, especially skilled at making traditional German dishes. She would cook up delicious stews, meats, and pies for the rich and was often allowed to bring leftovers home to feed Henry and Lou. She would also take home laundry from the mansions where she worked, wash the clothes at home, and bring them back the next day for extra money.

As a toddler, little Lou often went along with his mother on the trolley cars as she went back and forth from their tiny apartment to the sprawling houses where she cooked and cleaned. More than once, he fell asleep among baskets full of laundry, lulled by the rocking of the trolley cars.

❝ *Louie was always a good boy.* **❞**

—GEHRIG'S MOTHER

Lou's mother was very proud of her only child and was determined that he would have every chance to succeed in life. "He's the only big egg I have in my basket," she said. "He's the only one of four who lived, so I want him to have the best." When Lou was five years old, Christina had saved up enough money to move the family to a better neighborhood called Washington Heights. Here Lou could get a better education and have more fresh air and room to play. The neighborhood also happened to be very close to Hilltop Park—where the Highlanders baseball team, later known as the Yankees, played their home games.

Although Christina was proud of her German roots, she wanted to raise her son like he was just another American boy. She knew that for him to succeed in life, he would have to fit in. Although German was her first language, she always spoke English to him when he was young. He was speaking the language fluently by the age of five, but because his parents had thick accents, he spoke with an accent as well. Germans were a minority in the Gehrigs' new neighborhood, and when Lou started school, the kids teased him for the funny, slow way he talked, calling him the Dumb Dutchman or Heinie—a slang term for German people.

Lou was shy by nature and, like any kid, hated being teased. Unfortunately, he was an easy target. Because money was scarce, he often had to wear hand-me-down clothes that never fit his huge frame just right. He was bulky, awkward, and shabbily dressed—not a good combination for a kid who just wants to fit in. In grammar school (at that time, grammar school went from first grade to eighth grade), Lou was a good student, but he struggled to find a place where he belonged. He found it on the playground.

 As a kid, Lou loved Western movies.

Lou excelled at every sport and game imaginable. From football to soccer to basketball to running to marbles, Lou could do it all, but baseball quickly became his favorite sport. It was America's pastime, and Lou saw it as a way to become friends with the American kids. He was still teased, but it was tough to put down a kid who could whack the ball over the fence every time he came to bat. Lou's power was already paying off.

Lou's favorite baseball team was the New York Giants, who won the National League (NL) pennant three years in a row (1911–1913) while Lou was in grammar school. He also idolized an infielder for the Pittsburgh Pirates named Honus Wagner—a German American player who was nicknamed the "Flying Dutchman." Lou felt like he could relate to Wagner, his fellow countryman. He would read about Pittsburgh's games in the papers and was in awe as Wagner racked up hits and runs batted in (RBIs). Thanks to Wagner, Lou began dreaming of playing professional baseball one day. If that big German guy could do it, maybe Lou could, too!

The Yankees—then known as the Highlanders—played their first season in New York in 1903, the same year Lou Gehrig was born.

Lou was, after all, the biggest and strongest kid in his class. Aside from playing baseball, football, and soccer when they were in season, Lou also joined his school's track team as a shot-putter.

Henry Gehrig was proud of his son's strength, and when Lou was about ten years old, his dad started to bring him to the local German gyms, called turnvereins. At the gym, Lou would work out with his father, lifting weights and practicing on gymnastic equipment. Until then Henry had never been the most attentive father. Lou was much closer to his mother, who listened to his tales from the playground and helped with his homework, while his father was often out with his friends or trying to find work. But the turnvereins gave Henry an opportunity to spend time with his son and share something he loved.

Henry often felt out of touch with Lou, who was growing up to be such an Americanized boy. One year for Christmas, Lou's dad bought him a baseball glove in an attempt to bond with Lou, but he knew little about baseball and bought him a right-handed catcher's glove. Lou was a left-handed pitcher and fielder. Still, Lou appreciated the effort. He loved his dad and understood that he was just trying to take an interest in Lou's life.

Meanwhile Lou's mother worked longer and longer hours to help keep the family afloat, and ten-year-old Lou decided it was time for him to pitch in. Each day after school, he would deliver laundry and food to her customers, which earned him a bit of extra money as well—all of which he'd give to his mom.

Once when Lou was little, he got very sick, and his mother told him to stay home from school on his own. After she went to work, Lou got up and went to school. He just couldn't imagine missing a day.

Lou's mother was especially proud of her son's responsible nature. She loved him fiercely and wanted him to have a better life than she and his father did. She dreamed that Lou would become an engineer one day, so she ran a tight ship, making sure that Lou did all his homework and excelled in school. And even though he wasn't quite sure what it meant to be an engineer, Lou would do it if it was what his mother wanted for him. All he wanted was to be able to care for her one day as she had done for him all his life.

A dedicated student, Lou never missed a day of grammar school, and in 1917 he graduated from Public School (PS) 132 with a perfect attendance record. Even with all the hard work, he did manage to squeeze in some fun as well, having snowball fights with his friends in the winter and swimming with them in the Hudson River in the summer. He played billiards like a pro and challenged his friends to footraces on the sidewalks. He'd do just about anything to stay outside and stay active. Lou was an athlete by nature.

Somehow, between helping his mother, doing his school-work, and playing with his friends, Lou also managed to find time to play on the local baseball team. When he was twelve years old, his squad won the championship of the Parks Department League. It was the first time Lou Gehrig's name appeared in the newspaper.

Chapter Two

Another Babe?

In 1918 kids like Lou Gehrig didn't go to high school. When a boy from a working-class New York family graduated from grade school at age fourteen, he got his working papers and found a job. He brought home pay to help out the family. And when Lou graduated from PS 132, he was ready to do just that. But Christina Gehrig wouldn't have it.

Lou's mom was still dreaming of a better life for her son, so she enrolled him in the High School of Commerce, hoping that he would make something out of himself. She wanted him

In high school, Lou's least favorite class was typing because he was always making tons of mistakes. Why? His fingers were too big for the keys.

to buckle down and study, so that's what Lou did. He became so obsessed with doing well in school and making his mother proud, he decided that he wasn't even going to play sports in high school. Homework would be his life. This resolution didn't last very long.

Whenever Lou hit the practice fields to play with his friends, the adults watching could see he was a born star. One day during that first year of high school, Lou was out there with the rest of his classmates and he booted a soccer ball clear across the field. Everyone—including Commerce High's soccer coach—was stunned at the distance the ball flew. The coach asked Lou to join the team. Even though Lou had promised himself he would do nothing but study, the temptation to play was just too great. Sports were his first love, and here was a coach practically begging him to join a team!

Lou asked his mother if he could play soccer. At first she said no, but Lou promised that the team wouldn't get in the way of his schoolwork. Christina, when it came down to it, loved her only son and couldn't keep him from doing something he obviously wanted to do so badly. She gave in, and Lou joined the soccer team as a halfback. The team went on to win three straight championships.

But even though he was back on the playing field, where he felt like he belonged, Lou was still out of place at Commerce High.

For one thing, he was always low on cash. His family had to scrounge to pay the five-cent trolley car fare that got him to and from school. While the other boys in his class were able to buy sodas or ice cream after classes, Lou could never join in. So instead of hanging out after school and being a kid, Lou would go to work for a local butcher or grocer and pick up odd jobs wherever he could. The money didn't go to buying sodas, however. He always gave his earnings to his mother to help out at home.

Lou was also still big and awkward, with ill-fitting clothes. Not only that, but World War I was about to break out and many Americans were learning to hate Germany—a country that would be an enemy to the United States in the war. Lou was the victim of anti-German prejudice, which only isolated him more. Kids called Lou names and thought all German people were violent and aggressive. Lou had never even been to Germany, but he had to endure mean remarks about his heritage every day.

Then, when Lou was fifteen, his father became very ill. He couldn't even work when there *was* work to be had. His mother, who was still working odd jobs here and there, decided she needed something more permanent. She got a job working as a cook and housekeeper at a fraternity at Columbia University. When Henry finally got well, Christina got him a position at the fraternity house as a janitor. It was a good time for the Gehrig family. For the first time, both of Lou's parents had regular jobs.

During the summer between Lou's sophomore and junior years at Commerce High, Lou got a job working for the Otis Elevator Company in Yonkers. The company had a baseball team, and Lou joined up. He was a lefty pitcher and sometimes played infield. He was so good that one of his teammates recommended he try out for a real team—one that would pay him to play ball.

This sounded good to Lou. Back then lots of semipro teams existed in the New York area. He tried out for the Minqua Baseball Club and made it. The team would play other clubs in the New York area and in New Jersey. Each team was guaranteed thirty-five dollars a game, with five dollars going to the pitcher. Five dollars was a huge amount of money for a kid like Lou, and he loved bringing home his earnings to his mother. He felt like he was really contributing to his family for the first time. And he was doing it by playing baseball.

 As a teenager, Lou's baseball glove, though old and tattered, was his most prized possession.

Still, no one in the Gehrig family ever thought that playing ball would be something Lou could or would do for a living. He was going to graduate from high school, go to college, and become an engineer. That was his mother's plan. But in June 1920, when Lou was about to turn seventeen, something happened that would change the plan for good.

Once his mother had consented to let Lou play soccer, it had been easy to get her permission for Lou to join the football and baseball teams as well. Lou was stellar at every sport, of course. But that June he solidified himself as a baseball star.

Lou and his teammates on the Commerce High baseball team won the New York City championship. The *New York Daily News* thought it might be fun to see how New York's best high school players would stack up against Chicago's best, so they sponsored an intercity game. The High School of Commerce team would be going to Chicago to play Lane Technical High School at famous Wrigley Field, home of the Chicago Cubs.

Lou couldn't have been more psyched. He'd never been out of New York, and he was being offered a train trip with all his friends to Chicago to play ball at a major league park! He ran home to tell his mother about it and to ask her permission, but her reaction put a damper on his high spirits. Christina told Lou there was no way he was going to Chicago. Baseball was a silly pastime. He had work to do. There was no use in wasting his time playing a stupid game.

Lou was usually a good kid who didn't argue with his mother, but this time he couldn't keep his mouth shut. This was the opportunity of a lifetime, and he fought for it. The argument lasted for hours, and Lou's coach finally had to personally assure Lou's mom that he would take care of her son on the trip. It turned out that Christina wasn't worried so much about Lou wasting his time as she was worried about her only son's safety. Mrs. Gehrig was finally convinced, and she allowed Lou to go.

❝If you happened to play in a class game against him and he knocked the ball over your head, you just ran after it. I know you didn't console yourself by saying, 'That's the future Gehrig of the Yankees.' You were simply glad when he wasn't at bat.❞

—HIGH SCHOOL CLASSMATE LINCOLN WERDEN

It was an amazing experience for Lou—being away from home for the first time, riding in a sleeper train with his friends, eating dinner in the dining car, staying in a hotel. It was his first taste of freedom. Lou even got to meet former president William Taft, who happened to be on the train. Taft met with all of the boys on the team and told them, "I'm looking forward to seeing you boys play." The teenage Lou felt like a real celebrity.

Ten thousand people showed up at Wrigley Field to watch the High School of Commerce boys take on the players from Lane Tech High. At first it didn't look like Lou was going to give

19

them much to talk about. He went to bat five times without recording a hit. Even so, Commerce High was winning the game 8–6 in the ninth inning. His school seemed to have the game in hand, so Lou didn't have much to worry about when he approached the plate. But Lou was a team player, and he wanted to contribute if he could. The bases were loaded, and Lou hoped to drive in at least one run.

The first pitch was a strike. Lou didn't even swing at it. But when the second pitch came over the plate, Lou did swing—*hard*. The bat hit the ball with a resounding *crack*, and the ball lifted up over right field, cleared the bleachers, and landed on the porch of a house across the street. The crowd went crazy. Sixteen-year-old Lou Gehrig had just hit a grand slam in a major league ballpark!

❝ *Gehrig's blow would have made any big leaguer proud, yet it was walloped by a boy who hasn't yet started to shave.* ❞

—CHICAGO TRIBUNE, ABOUT LOU'S GRAND SLAM IN THE
COMMERCE VS. LANE TECH GAME

Lou grinned as he ran around the bases. It was a dream come true. Commerce won the game 12–6 and returned to New York as heroes. They were met at Grand Central Station by more than five thousand fans and a marching band that paraded them up Park Avenue. The New York papers ran photos of the team and play-by-play stories of each inning. One headline read: "Louis Gehrig Hits Ninth-Inning Homer With Bases Loaded." The *New York Times* said he was the Babe Ruth of the high schools.

Lou was astounded by all the attention. Who knew people cared so much about high school athletics? About him? But he was soon to find out that a lot of people cared about his talents.

Chapter | Three

Lou Lewis

Lou had become a minor celebrity in New York and Chicago, but school wasn't over yet. He still had to complete his senior year at Commerce High and figure out what he was going to do next. The family dream was still in place. Lou was expected to become an engineer. The only question was, how? The Gehrigs didn't have enough money to send Lou to college, and Lou's grades weren't high enough to get him an academic scholarship. Back in 1921, athletic scholarships were very rare. Lou's family didn't even consider his talents on the field as a ticket to get into school.

Fortunately, a man at Columbia University by the name of Bobby Watt was way ahead of them. He was the athletic director at the school, and Columbia hadn't been doing well in sports lately. Lou had made a name for himself not only in baseball, but in high school football as well. Watt saw Lou as a double threat—someone who could bring both Columbia's football and baseball teams out of the basement.

Both Lou's parents were still working at Columbia. Watt approached them and told them he could set up Lou with some entry-level courses. If he passed those courses and the college board exams, Lou would be admitted into the school with a full football scholarship. Lou's parents were ecstatic. Thanks to Lou's athletic talent, he was going to get to study for that engineer's degree.

Lou took the classes, worked hard as always, and passed the required tests. He was going to go to Columbia, one of the best schools in the country. His mother couldn't have been more proud, and Lou couldn't have been happier.

The summer before his freshman year at Columbia, Lou met a couple of scouts from the New York Giants—his favorite baseball team. Their names were Arthur Irwin and Art Devlin. They had seen Lou play at Commerce and offered him a tryout with the Giants. Lou would be going to school in the fall, but he figured he could earn some money playing baseball that summer. His family needed it. And besides, this was the Giants! He would be trying out for John McGraw, one of the greatest managers of all time. Lou couldn't pass that up.

Unfortunately, the Giants had been doing poorly, and McGraw, a man with a bad temper, was in a lousy mood on the day of Lou's tryout. Lou made one error in the field, and McGraw threw a fit, telling Devlin to get the kid out of there. He didn't even care that Lou had hit a number of balls into the stands.

Devlin didn't want to give up on Lou, so instead he got Lou a place with a Class A Eastern League team (similar to a minor league team) in Hartford, Connecticut. Lou didn't want to live away from his mother and father, but it was good money and a chance to play ball, so he went. His mother didn't object as long as he brought home his paycheck and was ready to start school in the fall. Devlin told Lou that while he was in Hartford, he should play under the name Lou Lewis. This made Lou suspicious. Was he doing something wrong? Was there some rule against college athletes playing baseball for money? Devlin assured Lou that there was no such rule, and Lou believed him. Devlin was an authority figure, and Lou trusted him.

Within days of his arrival in Hartford, "Lou Lewis" was being compared to Babe Ruth. The team won eight of the thirteen games they played while Lou was there. He batted .261 and hit two triples and a double. Lou was having fun, playing ball, and making decent money. Everything was great.

Then Andy Coakley, the baseball coach at Columbia, found out that Lou Lewis was actually Lou Gehrig. He took a train up to Hartford and brought Lou home. It turned out that playing for money *was* against collegiate rules. Lou had learned the hard way that he shouldn't trust everyone. His entire collegiate career was suddenly in jeopardy.

Luckily, Bobby Watt was able to smooth things over with the other schools Columbia played against. He explained that Lou had made a mistake but that he hadn't realized what he was doing was wrong. Lou could have been barred from college athletics for life, but the other schools agreed to a lesser sentence. Lou was barred from football for one season and from baseball for two seasons. He would start at Columbia as a regular student, not a student-athlete.

This sentence wouldn't keep Lou from practicing his heart out and keeping in shape. He could be seen most afternoons hitting balls, punting out on the football field, or running laps on the track. He wanted to be ready when he started with the teams.

At Columbia, Lou joined the Phi Delta Theta fraternity, but he was still treated poorly. Later in life, Lou never forgave Columbia for the way he was treated there, and when the school and fraternity tried to capitalize on his fame, he never helped them do so.

In the meantime, however, Columbia was not the most welcoming place. Most of the students were wealthy boys from respected families who could look forward to an easy road in life. They looked down on Lou. To them he was just a big oaf whose parents were the hired help at one of the fraternities. Lou tried to ignore them and concentrated on studying. He spent a lot of time alone in his first year and looked forward to getting back into sports, where he belonged.

And once Lou got back on the field, everyone knew about it. On the Columbia football team, he played as a running back, a guard, a lineman, *and* a punter. In his very first game against Ursinus College, he scored two touchdowns. In his second game, he contributed on defense, helping the team to hold Amherst to only six points. Then Columbia rolled over New York University (NYU). In each game, Lou played on both sides of the ball, which meant he hardly ever got a break.

"He was a battler. On the football field Lou worked with everything he had," said his teammate Robert Pulleyn. But just wait until baseball season.

Lou was a quadruple threat on the baseball team as well. He played lefty pitcher, first base, and in the outfield. Plus he had that great habit of smashing the ball out of the park. Coach Coakley sometimes even shifted Lou's position around during the same game, just to keep the other team guessing. In 1923, his first season on the team, Lou played in nineteen games. He played pitcher in eleven of them, first base in ten of them, and right field in one.

On April 18, 1923, the very day that Yankee Stadium opened, Lou struck out seventeen batters as Columbia played Williams. It was a school record that wasn't even *tied* until 1968. Columbia lost, but the feat was enough to make headlines anyway. "Gehrig Strikes Out Seventeen Batters, but Columbia Nine Loses to Williams by 5 to 1" read the *New York Tribune*'s headline. Other newspaper stories that year called Gehrig "the biggest star in college baseball" and "another Babe Ruth."

At the end of the season, he had twenty-four runs, twenty-eight hits, seven home runs, and five stolen bases. The stolen bases might have been the most surprising statistic. Lou was so big, no one believed he could be fast enough to steal—but he proved everyone wrong.

Even with all his time spent on the playing fields, Lou buckled down at school and managed to pull off a C average. His classmates recalled that he was always a hard worker and was prepared when called on in class. But would his grades be high enough for him to get an undergraduate degree in engineering?

Lou's favorite class in college was literature because the professor made the class fun and told hilarious stories.

Near the end of April, the Columbia baseball team traveled to New Brunswick, New Jersey, to play against Rutgers. A Yankee scout by the name of Paul Krichell came out to see the game and was impressed when Lou hit two balls into the trees around the ball field. He thought he might have found a player, but the game could have been a fluke. He went to see Gehrig play against NYU two days later at Columbia just to be sure. The game was tied 2–2 in the ninth inning when Lou came up to bat against Walter Huntzinger—the best college pitcher in the East. Lou slammed the ball out of the park and untied the game.

❝I did not go there to look at Gehrig. I did not even know what position he played. But he played in the outfield against Rutgers and socked a couple of balls a mile. I sat up and took notice. I saw a tremendous youth, with powerful arms and terrific legs. I said . . . 'Here is a kid who can't miss.'❞

—PAUL KRICHELL

Krichell was convinced. In fact, he was so excited that he dashed into the locker room after the game, walked right up to Lou, and introduced himself.

"I'm Paul Krichell," he said. "I scout for the Yankees. Have you signed with any major league ball club yet?"

Lou was so surprised, he could barely speak. "Why, no," he answered.

Then Krichell asked Lou if he'd like to play for the Yankees. Lou said what any other bright-eyed nineteen-year-old ballplayer would have said in the same situation: "Are you serious?"

The very next day, Lou met with Yankees general manager Ed Barrow, who offered Lou a contract. Lou would get $2,000 for the remainder of the season plus a $1,500 signing bonus. This was huge money for Lou. At the time, his mother was suffering from pneumonia, and his father was ailing again. His family needed the money, and it seemed like a lucky break. Lou knew that his mother wouldn't be happy with the idea of her son playing professional baseball and giving up on engineering, but he also knew he had to take care of her. So Lou Gehrig, ever the good son, signed on to become a New York Yankee.

B *The money they put before me was enough to turn any kid's head. I was still not sure I wanted to go into baseball as a steady profession, but I decided to grab what I could of it.* c

—LOU GEHRIG

29

Chapter | Four

Earning His Stripes

In June 1923, Lou Gehrig took the subway to Yankee Stadium with his glove and his spikes wrapped in a newspaper. Nothing fancy for this rookie. No one would have guessed he was on his way to baseball stardom.

Lou was understandably nervous as he walked into the stadium and through the clubhouse. This was a big deal for the shy, awkward twenty-year-old. When the team's trainer, Doc Woods, stopped in the clubhouse to introduce Lou to Babe Ruth, Lou was speechless. This man was a legend. Lou had followed his career for years. And here they were, standing in the same room.

By the time Miller Huggins, the Yankees' manager, took Lou out to the field for a little batting practice, Lou was practically shaking with nervousness. Some of the team's heaviest hitters came out to watch him. His audience included Babe, first baseman Wally Pipp, shortstop Everett Scott, and second baseman Aaron Ward.

Trying to stay calm, Lou chose a bat—a nice heavy one. What he didn't know was that he was picking up Babe's favorite bat.

A big league star like Babe Ruth could have stepped in and told Lou to lay off his bat, but Ruth didn't. He was more interested to see if Lou could swing the thing.

In his nervousness, Lou swung at and missed the first few pitches and then hit a couple of grounders. His powerful swing and arcing homers were nowhere in sight. The Yankee team members who hovered around the batting cage weren't impressed. But a couple of Lou's friends from Columbia had come to cheer for him, and they began shouting from the bleachers. "Show that big guy, Lou!" they yelled, meaning Babe Ruth.

Lou was buoyed by his friends' support. He took his stance, watched the ball, and swung. This time he connected, and the ball went sailing over the field, landing in the bleachers off right field. At the time, those bleachers were known as "Ruthville" because Babe Ruth knocked so many homers that way. The pitcher threw more fastballs over the plate, and Lou slammed more home runs out of the park. Miller Huggins was impressed. Apparently Paul Krichell had been right when he'd said he was bringing in the next Babe.

Unfortunately for Lou, the Yankees were a tight group. They had won two straight pennants, meaning they had been the best team in the American League for two straight years and gone to the World Series. (The team that wins the American

League pennant plays the team that wins the National League pennant in the series.) Plus the Yankees had Wally Pipp, an excellent player, at first base. Lou's fielding wasn't as spectacular as his hitting, so Huggins decided that Lou should play with a lesser team for a while to perfect his game. The Yankees had made an arrangement with the Hartford Senators—the same team "Lou Lewis" had played for a couple of years back. Under the arrangement, the Senators agreed to take on rookies for the Yankees so they could have more playing time and improve their skills. Once again Lou was shipped off to Hartford to play.

Lou's mother, who was already unhappy that he'd chosen to play a game for a living, was upset that he wouldn't be playing with the Yankees. She didn't understand the system and thought Huggins's plan was an insult. But Lou knew that Huggins was right. He was going to need some work if he was going to play up to the Yankees' high standards. And his mother stopped complaining when Lou started sending home his hefty paycheck.

Lou's mother didn't appreciate her son getting shipped off to a lesser team, but when she heard it was Hartford, she felt better. To her, Hartford sounded like Harvard—which was as good as Columbia.

Still, Lou did get into one Yankee game before he left for Hartford. On June 16, 1923, the Yankees played the St. Louis Browns. Gehrig was sent in to replace Wally Pipp in the ninth inning, but it was so late in the game that nothing interesting happened. Lou would get a lot more playing time once he was in Hartford.

So Lou found himself in a Hartford Senators uniform again, but this time he didn't do as well on the diamond. He fell in with a rough crowd and slumped at the plate. Paddy O'Connor, the coach of the Hartford team, was understandably upset. He thought he was getting a star and instead he got a lazy stinker. He called Paul Krichell, who knew that O'Connor's description didn't sound like Lou. Krichell went up to Hartford and found Lou sad and listless. He was even talking about quitting. When Krichell asked Lou what was wrong, Lou told him that he just didn't think he could live up to what was expected of him in Hartford. Finally Krichell understood. All the local papers had run articles before Lou's arrival, excited about their great new player. It was too much pressure for Lou, who wanted to do so well.

Krichell gave Lou a pep talk. He told him to stop hanging around with the guys who were a bad influence and to remember what was important. He was a ballplayer, and it was time to start playing ball.

Lou's Hartford teammates nicknamed him "Buster" because he could bust the ball with his bat.

After Krichell's visit, a new Lou Gehrig took the field in Hartford. He had sixty-nine hits and hit twenty-four home runs, at one point hitting seven homers in seven days. The fans started to support him, and he ended his time in Hartford with a .304 batting average.

Meanwhile Lou was making good money but still living like a pauper. He sent almost his entire paycheck home to his parents and even bought them a house in New Rochelle, New York, so that they could move out of the city. Just as Lou had always dreamed, he was finally paying his mother back for supporting him all those years. He might not be an engineer, but she saw the kind of money Lou could make on the baseball diamond. His mother never complained about his choice of career again.

In September, Miller Huggins called Lou back to Yankee Stadium to see how he would fare in the big leagues. The Yankees were already guaranteed the pennant because they had won so many games that no one else could catch up with them. Huggins figured that putting Lou in couldn't hurt them now, no matter how he played. Lou's first game back in a Yankee uniform wasn't stellar. He came in to pinch-hit and struck out against the Washington Senators. He did better in his second game, replacing Pipp at first base in late innings and hitting a double that tied the game.

Lou started at first base in his third game so that Wally Pipp could rest and get ready for the World Series. In this game, Lou made an error at first base, and the pitcher, "Bullet" Joe Bush, shouted at him for being so stupid. Lou was visibly upset by the outburst and actually had to blink back tears. He was still a young man and wasn't used to so much pressure. Still, he made up for his mistake, hitting a double that scored three runs to tie the game, then coming home on the next hit to score the winning run. Bush didn't yell at Lou much after that.

On September 27, 1923, the Yankees went to Boston to play their last game of the regular season. Wally Pipp tripped on his way off the train and injured his ankle, so Lou got to start. That day he hit his very first major league home run.

In the 1923 season, Lou came to bat twenty-six times as a Yankee. He had eleven hits and one home run.

With Pipp injured, Huggins wanted Lou to play first base in the World Series. Lou couldn't have been more excited. Substitutions were normally not allowed so late in the season, but sometimes exceptions were made, especially when players were injured. To get Lou in, Huggins had to get permission from the manager of the opposing team. The Yankees were playing against the New York Giants, so Huggins went to John McGraw, the Giants' manager, to see if he would allow the substitution.

McGraw was the same man who had booted Lou off his field two years before, telling Art Devlin he was no good. He was bitter over missing his chance at Lou, who looked like he was going to turn into a great player. He angrily refused the substitution, forcing Pipp to play with his bum ankle. After this incident, Lou had even more reason to dislike John McGraw, but there was nothing he could do. He sat on the bench and watched his team beat the Giants in the World Series. It seemed McGraw's tactic to make sure the Yanks had a weak first baseman hadn't worked.

In 1924 Lou attended his first spring training camp in New Orleans, Louisiana. Players didn't get paid until the season started, so when he arrived, he had only fourteen dollars to his name and carried a cardboard suitcase. While most of the team was living it up, going out to fancy restaurants and staying in posh hotels, Lou was practically penniless. He would practice all day, then scrounge for odd jobs at night, washing dishes at local restaurants and doing whatever else he could for money.

Finally Miller Huggins found out what was going on and gave Lou a hundred dollars so that he could stop looking for work and start concentrating on baseball. He also set Lou up in a hotel room with two of his older teammates, Benny Bengough, a catcher, and Hinkey Haines, an outfielder.

Lou got along with his roommates but found that he was the butt of a lot of jokes at training camp. He wanted to save his money, so he never spent time with the team outside of practice. His teammates thought this behavior was snobbish, antisocial, and just plain weird. They teased him for being a tightwad and for being unsophisticated. Not only that, but all rookies were abused on the field by the veterans. Some even threw rocks at the rookies while they were batting. Lou once showed up to practice to find his favorite bat sawed into pieces. This behavior made Lou heartsick. He didn't understand how anyone could be so hurtful and mean.

One pitcher, Carl Mays, was particularly awful to Lou. His gibes and teasing were incessant. One afternoon, when Lou finally couldn't take it anymore, he offered to fight Mays. Mays took one look at Lou's huge legs and arms and his great height and backed off.

Meanwhile Lou kept his head down and worked his hardest to improve his fielding skills. Miller Huggins had begun to really admire the soft-spoken Lou and his dedication to the game. Huggins took Lou under his wing, working with him personally on the field. Under Huggins's watchful eye, Lou steadily improved, making fewer and fewer errors at practice.

❝ *The ballplayer who loses his head, who can't keep his cool, is worse than no ballplayer at all.* ❞

—LOU GEHRIG

Even so, Wally Pipp remained the Yankees' starting first baseman. He was still an excellent player and was back in top condition. When the season started, Lou was once again sent to Hartford so that he would get playing time and stay in shape. Lou went willingly, but after last year's taste of the big leagues he was more determined than ever to make it back to the Yankees.

Chapter Five

The Greatest Team of All Time

L ou played well in Hartford in 1924. He played in 134 games and had 186 hits, thirty-seven of them home runs. He had an especially good day on his twenty-first birthday, hitting a home run, a triple, and a double and helping his team to a 9–8 win over a team from Worcester, Massachusetts. In 1924 he also had twenty-three errors in the field, however. He'd been working hard, but he still needed some practice at first base.

Again Huggins brought Lou to New York for the last few regular season games, but Lou didn't get to play much. The Yankees lost the pennant to the Washington Senators, and their season was over.

In December of that year, a rumor spread that Lou was about to be traded from the Yankees. Reporters suggested that his fielding was still no good and that he would never be able to take Wally Pipp's job. The story was reported in some New York papers, and Lou started to worry that it might be true. Was Miller Huggins, a man whom he had come to view as a second father, going to trade him?

Huggins quickly put the rumors to rest, calling the story "the silliest thing that was ever written." When the Yankees traveled to their new spring training camp in St. Petersburg, Florida, Lou was still with them.

The year 1925 turned out to be a crazy one for the Yankees. First Babe Ruth got violently ill on his way back from training camp. Many reporters speculated that Ruth's partying had finally caught up to him, but the sickness turned out to be a curable stomach problem. Nevertheless, Ruth was out for the first couple of months of the season. By the time he returned to his team on June 1, the Yankees had racked up more losses than wins.

But June 1 turned out to be a significant day for Lou. Huggins sent in Lou Gehrig to pinch-hit for Pee Wee Wanninger in the eighth inning. All Lou wanted to do was contribute to the team. Unfortunately, he didn't get a hit, and he figured he'd be benched again for a while. But the very next day, everything changed.

At batting practice on June 2, Wally Pipp was hit in the head by a pitch and went down unconscious. He was sent to the hospital, where he would stay for two weeks. With Pipp gone, Lou took over as the first base starter. Huggins placed him sixth in the batting order. At this time, Babe Ruth was batting cleanup (fourth).

"Before I went in for Pipp, I was so discouraged at my slim prospect for getting regular work at first that I asked Hug to try me in the outfield, which already had Ruth, Combs, and Meusel in it," Lou said. Huggins didn't put him in the outfield, but he sympathized with his young player's desire to get off the bench. Although it was a bad break for Wally Pipp, Lou must have been relieved to finally get his shot.

It wasn't easy for Lou, however. His fielding was still bad, and he often made mistakes during games. Even Huggins, Lou's biggest fan, occasionally exploded at him. The press also took an instant dislike to Lou, not just because he was messing up on the field but because he avoided interviews as much as possible. Still shy and soft-spoken, Lou didn't know how to work the press and the fans like the boisterous Babe Ruth did. As a result, no matter how well Lou played, Babe continued to dominate the headlines.

But not all of Babe's headlines were good. Once he got back in action on the field, he also got back in action in the city. He was partying all night, coming to practices and games late, and talking back to his coaches and the team manager. His behavior infuriated Huggins, who would rather have had a million players with Lou's temperament. Huggins and Babe fought, sometimes publicly, and Huggins sat Babe out of games, then suspended him entirely.

With so much turmoil on the team, the Yankees were slumping badly. No one seemed to notice that Lou was out there racking up a couple of firsts. His first stolen base came on June 24, when he stole home—a rare feat. He had his first grand slam on July 23. Lou ended the season with twenty home runs, sixty-eight RBIs, 129 hits, and a batting average of .295. The Yankees, however, had an awful season. Ruth eventually apologized to Huggins and returned to work, but he couldn't lift his team out of the hole they'd dug for themselves. They finished the season in seventh place, twenty-eight and a half games out of first, with sixty-nine wins and eighty-five losses. The media and the fans predicted that the great Yankees were through.

In the off-season, Miller Huggins had replaced a lot of old players with new blood, and the whole team seemed reenergized. Ruth had cleaned up his act and was ready to play, and Lou had rededicated himself to improving his skills at first base.

Lou and Babe quickly convinced the fans that they were not about to repeat their 1925 performance. In the very first game of the 1926 season, Lou stole home and at the same time, Babe stole third. Double-steal plays were almost unheard of, but Lou and Babe sent a clear message—the Yankees were going to be the team to beat.

The team blew through the season, happy to have the awful 1925 stats behind them. Lou had been batting third all year, but he started hitting so well that Huggins switched the lineup, putting Babe third, with Lou batting cleanup. This one-two punch of power hitters became feared across the league. Pitchers hated trying to pitch through Babe and Lou. They were just too good. If a pitcher walked Babe to save themselves a home run, he would then have to face Lou, who would just as likely hit a home run. Other teams held their breath whenever a pitcher took on Babe and Lou, just hoping for a miracle—that no one would score.

That year, even though he was just twenty-three years old, Lou emerged as a role model for the team. His teammates admired his responsible nature and his hard work. Lou's mother, meanwhile, became a favorite with the team. Whenever Lou brought his friends home from the stadium, Lou's mom would be ready with her specialty snacks (including pickled eels!) and a warm welcome. Babe Ruth, in particular, loved Mrs. Gehrig's cooking and could often be found at her kitchen table, ready to eat. The team took to calling Lou's parents "Mom" and "Pop" just like Lou did. After a while the names stuck, and even the press started using the casual names to describe Lou's parents.

Lou's consecutive games-played streak earned him the nicknames "Iron Horse" and "Iron Man" in the papers.

The Yankees racked up ninety wins and just sixty-three losses that year, a nice improvement from a year before. They won the American League (AL) pennant and faced the St. Louis Cardinals in the World Series. This was Lou's first series as an active player, and he couldn't wait to take the field and help his team to victory.

Lou had a great series. He had eight hits, three RBIs, and two doubles. His batting average for the series was a solid .348.

The series was an up-and-down thrill ride for the team. In the first game, the Yankees won 2–1, and Lou himself drove in both runs. The Cardinals won the second and third games, 6–2 and 5–0. Then in the fourth game, Babe Ruth promised the press he'd hit two home runs. Instead he hit *three*. Lou contributed with a double, and the Yankees trounced the Cards 10–5. The fifth game went into extra innings, and the Yankees won 3–2 to move ahead three games to two. Unfortunately, it wasn't meant to be. The Cardinals won the last two games, 10–2 and 3–2, and left the Yankees disappointed.

The Yanks may have been down, but they were definitely not out. They came back in 1927 with a vengeance.

Before the season began, no one realized how powerful the Yankees batting order was going to be. Many baseball experts predicted the Philadelphia Athletics would win the AL pennant. But at the end of May, the Yankees beat the Athletics twice in a doubleheader (two games in a single day). They won the first game 10–3 and the second game 18–5. The Yanks hit six home runs, and in the first game, Lou almost hit for the cycle. (A cycle occurs when one player hits a home run, a triple, a double, and a single in one game. Lou missed only the single.) There wasn't much doubt which was the better team after that.

From June 1 to June 23, the Yankees won twenty of their twenty-four games. By midseason, they had an eleven and a half game lead in the AL. Meanwhile pitchers were quaking in the face of Babe Ruth and Lou Gehrig, who had started a home run derby of epic proportions. It seemed that every time Babe Ruth hit a homer, Lou would answer with his own. In July, Lou had twenty-eight home runs and Babe had twenty-six. They would remain close for the rest of the season until September, when Babe opened it up. He hit seventeen home runs in one month, while Lou hit just six. It was clear who was going to win the home run battle. Babe broke his own record of fifty-nine by hitting number sixty on September 30. Lou contributed with forty-seven, not a bad little number. And he didn't mind losing out on the battle to his friend and teammate Babe Ruth. He was just glad he and the "Sultan of Swat" were on the same team!

Batting behind Babe, who regularly cleared the bases with his homers, Lou still knocked in 175 runs. He finished the season with a .373 average, better than Babe's .356. He had 218 hits, fifty-two doubles, eighteen triples, and forty-seven home runs. In only his second full season in the majors, Lou Gehrig was elected the Most Valuable Player (MVP) of the year for the AL. (Babe, with his record-breaking sixty home runs, might have won if not for a rule that prevented players from winning the honor more than once in their career. Ruth had won in 1923.)

The New York Yankees team of 1927 is often called the "Greatest Team of All Time." They racked up 110 wins in 154 games, a team record that went untouched until 1998, when the Yanks won 114 games. The batting order of 1927 was nick-named "Murderer's Row." And it wasn't just Gehrig and Ruth doing the hitting. The Yankees team, including Earle Combs, Mark Koenig, Bob Meusel, Tony Lazzeri, and Joe Dugan, hit 158 home runs. The team with the second-most home runs for the season, the Philadelphia Athletics, had only fifty-six. That was fewer than Babe Ruth hit *by himself.*

The Yankees of 1927 were called the team of "Five O'Clock Lightning." Games started at three PM, and the Yankee rallies usually started up in the late innings, right about five o'clock.

In the 1927 World Series, the Yankees faced the Pittsburgh Pirates. They were a solid team but not nearly good enough to take the Yankees down. They almost caught a lucky break when Lou considered skipping the series. His mother had become seriously ill just before the series was about to begin, and Lou told Huggins he was thinking about staying home with her. His family, after all, had always come first. But Huggins convinced him that his teammates needed him, and Lou stayed with the team.

The series began in Pittsburgh. The first game was a tight one, but the Yankees pulled it out, winning 5–4. Lou contributed with a triple in the first inning. In the second game, the Yankees won 6–2, with Lou hitting a double in the third and batting in a run in the eighth. In game three, Lou hit a ball that fired through center field. Koenig and Combs scored, and Lou ran the bases as fast as he could, hoping for an in-the-park home run. Unfortunately, he was caught at home and called out. Still, the Yankees went on to win the game 8–1.

The Yankees led the series three games to none. Things were looking good. But could they do what had never been done before? Could they be the first American League team to sweep the World Series?

The fourth game was close, and it looked like the Pirates might actually pull out a win. But in the ninth inning, a Pirates pitcher named John Miljus threw a wild pitch, and the winning run came home. The Yankees beat the Pirates 4–3 and swept the series in four games. It was one for the history books.

Ruth and Gehrig had combined to knock in eleven of the Yankees' total nineteen runs. The two were truly the stars of the series, the stars of the entire season. It seemed as if nothing could stop them.

 In 1927 Lou's salary from the Yankees was $7,500. Babe Ruth's was a league-high $70,000.

Ever since Lou officially joined the Yankees starting lineup early in the 1925 season, he and Babe had been friends. Ruth respected Lou's batting ability and liked to have fun with the shy young fellow. Lou was in awe of Babe's athletic talents and his ability to be so casual with the press and the fans. They were social opposites, but they got along well, fishing together on days off and having dinner at Lou's parents' house. Even during their home run battle, Lou and Babe always supported each other, shaking hands whenever one of them crossed home after knocking one out of the park.

Still, there was no doubt that Babe Ruth was more popular with the fans and the press because of his outgoing nature. Some say it was tough for Lou to always be in his teammate's shadow, but if it was, Lou never showed it. He was happy to be winning and to be able to contribute to his team.

---

66 *The Babe is one fellow, and I'm another and I could never be exactly like him. I don't try, I just go on as I am in my own right.* 99

—LOU GEHRIG

After the 1927 season, however, Lou was also getting a lot of press. Everyone in America knew about Babe Ruth and Lou Gehrig and their fearsome bats. Even people who had never seen a professional baseball game before could read about their amazing plays in the newspaper or listen to them on the radio. As soon as the World Series was over, Babe Ruth's business manager, Christy Walsh, suggested that he and Lou try to capitalize on this countrywide fame.

Walsh decided that the best thing would be to send Lou and Babe on a barnstorming tour. Barnstorming was a slang term used to describe a tour that brought major league players to the midwestern and southern farming areas, where the people had never gotten to see the pros in action. At this time in history, major league baseball clubs were situated in and around big industrial cities, where there was money for stadiums and plenty of fans to buy tickets. Since the southern and midwestern states didn't have many of these metropolitan areas, it would be a while before teams sprouted up in places like Florida, Kansas, and Texas. Babe thought barnstorming was a great idea to make some extra money and to see the country. Lou was reluctant at first, not wanting to spend so much time away from home, but Babe worked on him in his animated way. It was going to be fun, and he assured Lou that he would bring home a big paycheck as well—more than he had made all year. Lou was finally convinced.

Chapter | Six

Ups and Downs

On October 11, just three days after the World Series sweep was complete, Lou and Babe left New York on a train from Penn Station. For three weeks they toured the country, meeting fans at train stations and playing with local players in sold-out parks. Babe's team was called "The Bustin' Babes" and Lou's team was called "The Larrupin' Lous." Each team was made up of local players and the one star. Imagine how exciting it must have been for farmers and workers to pitch against the great Lou Gehrig and Babe Ruth!

Everywhere Lou went, he was surprised and touched by the fans' enthusiasm. In San Jose, California, all twelve of the schools and most of the businesses closed down so that people could go to see the game. On October 29, more than 30,000 fans came to Wrigley Field in Los Angeles, California (designed to be like Wrigley Field in Chicago), to see the two stars slug it out.

For the first time, Lou realized just how famous he was.

By the time the three-week barnstorming tour was complete, Lou had racked up thirteen home runs and had recorded an amazing batting average of .618. Of course, that might have been because he was playing against amateurs, but it was still slightly better than Babe's .616. The two men might have had different outlooks on life and different batting techniques, but there was no denying they were both great players.

In the mid-twenties some newspapers dubbed Babe and Lou "the King and the Crown Prince" of baseball.

Lou and Babe continued their power hitting and kept the Yankees winning in 1928. The team won thirty-nine of their first forty-eight games. It looked like the Yankees and Murderer's Row were going to keep up the unbelievable pace of 1927. And they might have, if not for a number of injuries.

During the 1928 season, the Yankees' injury report could have been mistaken for the team roster. Almost everyone was ailing at some point or another. Third baseman Joe Dugan blew out his knee and was out for weeks. Herb Pennock, one of the team's best pitchers, hurt his arm and missed several games.

Babe Ruth suffered a charley horse toward the end of the season that had him limping visibly when he rounded bases. Combs, Meusel, Lazzeri, and Bengough were all out at different points in the season with different injuries. But worst of all, ace pitcher Urban Shocker, who had won eighteen games in 1927, had to retire early in the 1928 season because of a heart ailment. He died suddenly on September 9, much to the shock of Lou and his teammates, who didn't realize how very sick he was.

Lou, of course, wasn't immune to injuries, either. But he was known throughout his career for playing with broken fingers and sprained toes, even with severe headaches. (First basemen suffer a lot of broken fingers because so many outs are made at first base. A lot of balls come rocketing into first from all over the field.) If Lou had anything serious ailing him, his teammates would never know. As long as the Yankees needed him, he was out there play-ing. Lou contributed greatly during the 1928 season. He finished with a .374 batting average and twenty-seven home runs. He also led the league in RBIs for the second straight year, with 142.

&&*I can remember when Lou had a broken middle finger on his right hand. Every time he batted a ball it hurt him . . . but he always stayed in the game.*99

—TEAMMATE BILLY WERBER

Missing players were temporarily replaced throughout the season with men who didn't have as much experience, making for a messy roster and a lot of inconsistency. The Yankees ended up in a battle for first place with the Philadelphia Athletics. The Athletics had held first place briefly during the first week of September, and the Yankees would have to beat them in both games of a doubleheader to win the AL pennant. The games took place on September 9, 1928, the same day Urban Shocker passed away. As many as 80,000 fans packed the stands at Yankee Stadium to watch the matchup.

Pulling together to play their best, the Yankees showed their championship colors that day. Yankee pitcher George Pipgras shut out the A's in the first game, and Bob Meusel hit a grand slam in the second game to beat their rivals. The Yankees finished two and a half games up in first place and earned the right to face the St. Louis Cardinals in the World Series.

The Yankees went into the series looking for revenge. After losing to the Cards in 1926, they wanted payback.

The series started off at Yankee Stadium during the first week of October. In the first game, the Yankees beat the Cardinals 4–1, with Lou hitting a double and a single and knocking in two runs. In the first inning of the second game, Lou slammed the first pitch that came his way, sending a home run into the right-field bleachers and clearing the two men on base.

Energized, the Yankees went on to win the game 9–3.

In game three, which was played in St. Louis, Lou hit two homers, one of them an inside-the-park home run, and drove in three runs. The Yankees won 7–3. The following day, Lou hit his fourth home run of the series—the homer that put the Yankees ahead for the rest of the game. The Yankees won again with a score of 7–3 and recorded their second straight World Series sweep. Lou's batting average for the series was a stellar .545. He had six hits, drove in nine runs, and scored five runs himself.

Even though Lou had an incredible series, Babe Ruth was still regarded as the hero of the sweep. He had three home runs in the last game and recorded a series average of .625—the highest ever for a player in a four-game series. When the team returned to New York on October 10, Babe earned the loudest round of applause from the waiting fans. Still, Lou was happy that his team was back on top for the second year.

Lou's mom was one of his biggest supporters, coming to every game and practice she could attend. She even went along on road trips and often brought homemade food to the guys on the team so that they would still eat well while they were away.

At the beginning of the 1929 season, talk of the Yankees' dominance filtered throughout the country. Some people thought the league should intervene to break up the team to add a little balance. That way the Yankees wouldn't be able to roll to their third straight title. Another rumor started up that Lou was going to be traded, but Huggins quickly put it to rest. He wasn't going to break up his team. He liked it just the way it was—in winning form.

Unfortunately, 1929 didn't turn out to be the best year for the Yankees. They didn't roll over anyone. Lou had an off year, hitting only .300. He had thirty-four home runs, more than the year before, but his RBIs and his hits took a dip. Babe's home run production slowed down as well, and other members of the infamous Murderer's Row started to show their age. The team racked up eighty-eight wins and sixty-six losses but lost the pennant race to the dominant Athletics.

In 1929 the Yankees were the first team to make numbers a permanent part of their jerseys. Lou was given the number 4 because it was his position in the batting order.

The team took a big hit personally as well, suffering a loss that would affect Lou more than anyone. In late September, Miller Huggins, the Yankees' manager and the man whom Lou admired so much, was hospitalized with a rare infectious skin disease. He died suddenly on September 25 at the age of fifty.

"Next to my father and mother he was the best friend a boy could have," Lou said at the time. "There was never a more patient or pleasant man to work for. I can't believe he's gone."

The Yankees had the off-season to recover from the loss. Lou disliked these yearly vacations from baseball because he enjoyed playing so much, but he kept himself busy and physically fit by ice-skating and running. While many of his team members used those lazy months to party and pack on the pounds, Lou spent his free time either at home with his parents or obsessively conditioning his body. He even helped his teammate and friend Waite Hoyt shed a few pounds in the off-season by introducing him to speed skating.

That winter, while Lou was working out and staying fit, the Yankees hired a new manager. Bob Shawkey, the man who took over the team for the 1930 season, was not a big favorite of Lou's. In the spring of 1930, Shawkey traded a lot of Lou's teammates, including Koenig, Meusel, and Hoyt—three men Lou depended on and admired. But even though Lou didn't agree with these decisions, he kept his mouth shut. Managing wasn't his job, and, ever respectful of authority, he wasn't going to put in his two cents.

The Yankees ended up the 1930 season in third place, but Lou's numbers rebounded. He had a career-high 220 hits, 174 RBIs, and a batting average of .379. It wasn't enough to help the Yankees to the pennant, however, and once again the team started looking for a new manager.

Joe McCarthy, who had just been fired by the Chicago Cubs, was hired on as the Yankees' manager for the 1931 season. When the team reported for spring training that year, both Lou and his roommate and friend Bill Dickey took an instant liking to the new man in charge. McCarthy ran a tight ship with dress codes (suits were to be worn to and from each game), tough practices, and an insistence that his team arrive on time and practice late if needed. He even put a stop to card playing in the dugout, a practice that most of the Yankees indulged in, including Babe Ruth. McCarthy, of course, butted heads with Babe Ruth, who hated to be told what to do and was never good at keeping to schedules. But hardworking Lou appreciated McCarthy's professional approach to managing. Under his new leader, Lou ended up having a stellar year with forty-six home runs, 211 hits, and 184 RBIs. His home run numbers even tied with Babe's for most in the league.

Lou's grade-school portrait, taken in 1917 when he was fourteen years old.

Lou started playing baseball for Columbia in the spring of 1923, and by year's end he was a member of the New York Yankees.

At the plate, Lou used a tight batting stance and powerful arms to wallop fast-moving line drives out of the ballpark.

The 1927 infield: Gehrig (first base), Tony Lazzeri (second base), Mark Koenig (shortstop), and Joe Dugan (third base)

Though Lou struggled with his fielding skills early in his career, his dedicated practice helped him to become one of the best first basemen in Yankees' history.

Lou and Babe before their friendship ran into trouble at the end of Babe's career in 1934.

Eleanor Gehrig plants a kiss on her favorite baseball player, four years after they were married.

Lou shows off his powerful athletic ability as young Joe DiMaggio, who joined the team in 1936, holds the bat.

In a major league career spanning seventeen baseball seasons, the Iron Horse played 2,130 consecutive games and became a legend in his own time.

HENRY LOUIS GEHRIG
NEW YORK YANKEES · 1923 · 1939
HOLDER OF MORE THAN A SCORE OF
MAJOR AND AMERICAN LEAGUE RECORDS,
INCLUDING THAT OF PLAYING 2130
CONSECUTIVE GAMES. WHEN HE RETIRED
IN 1939, HE HAD A LIFE TIME BATTING
AVERAGE OF 340.

This plaque commemorating Lou's great accomplishments hangs in the Hall of Fame Gallery at the National Baseball Hall of Fame in Cooperstown, New York.

Lou actually would have won the home run title if not for a blunder by his teammate Lyn Lary. Late in the season, in a game against Washington with two outs, Lou hit a home run into the bleachers. It bounced out again, right into the glove of the center fielder. Lyn Lary, who had been on first base, started running but never saw that the ball had gone out of play. When he realized the ball was in the center fielder's glove, he figured that the ball had been caught, that Lou was out, and that the inning was over. Lary headed for the dugout, while Lou, who didn't see Lary leave, jogged around the bases. Because Lou technically got home before Larry did, Lou was called out. If not for the mishap, Lou would have had forty-seven homers.

While his teammates and McCarthy were mad at Lary for his mistake, Lou never blamed anyone for such things. Everyone made mistakes, and Lou had made a lot of them in his early years. Besides, forty-six homers was still the best in the league, even if he was tied with his teammate for the title.

The Yankees came in second place in the pennant race in 1931, finishing behind the Athletics, who won for the third

straight year. Lou, who hated losing and was often unapproach-
able for a good hour after a loss, was getting tired of missing out
on the pennant. Luckily, something was happening in his per-
sonal life that took the edge off the disappointment.

 In 1931 Lou hit three grand slams in four days.

Chapter Seven

Love and Marriage

Lou Gehrig had once been introduced to a beautiful young girl named Eleanor Twitchell during a game against the Chicago White Sox at Chicago's Comiskey Park. Although stunned by her beauty, he was still a shy and awkward young man and barely said hello before returning to the dugout. But three years after their first brief meeting, Lou was given a second chance with Eleanor.

During a road trip to Chicago in the middle of the 1931 season, Lou went to a party at a friend of a friend's apartment. Eleanor was a guest at the party, and Lou, who had grown more mature and self-confident, spent almost the entire night chatting with her. Whenever Eleanor broke away from their conversation to greet someone else or talk to other men, Lou couldn't take his eyes off her. He was falling in love.

That night Lou walked Eleanor home. Although he was too shy to give her a good-night kiss, he sent her a gift a week later, and Eleanor knew Lou liked her. The gift was a crystal necklace along with a romantic note. The necklace was a huge gesture coming from Lou, who was a notorious penny-pincher. Following that first note, he and Eleanor began writing to each other, speaking on the phone, and seeing each other whenever Lou was in Chicago with the team.

Then, early in the spring of 1932, while the season was still young, the Yankees traveled to Chicago. One morning of the road trip, Lou got Eleanor to play hooky from her job as a secretary and took her for breakfast at the famous Drake Hotel. Eleanor later wrote in her book *My Luke and I:* "I don't remember who proposed to whom. . . . We lingered over coffee for hours, then drove to my house to tackle whatever problems we'd find there." There were no problems, however. Eleanor's family was thrilled that the two were engaged. And that afternoon, Eleanor went to see her new fiancé play at Comiskey Park, where he hit a home run for her.

Lou's mother wasn't as pleased about the news as Eleanor's parents were. Lou was her only son, and the thought of losing him to another woman made her crazy. She came out to visit Eleanor in Chicago and complained about everything from her living arrangements to the restaurants to which she was taken. "The best way I can put it is that she lacked humor or ease to an alarming degree," Eleanor later wrote.

Lou's mother had a parrot that shouted baseball terms all day long.

Lou and Eleanor realized that they had their work cut out for them, but they weren't going to let Lou's mom scare them out of getting married. In September 1932, Eleanor moved to the East Coast. She was to stay at the Gehrigs' house with Lou and his parents while she and Lou looked for a place to live. Lou's mother basically terrorized Eleanor once she was under the same roof with her. She thought Eleanor was just a society girl who wouldn't be able to cook or clean or care for her son in the way that she, his mother, could. Eleanor tried to grin and bear the insults, but it was a difficult living situation for everyone.

Meanwhile the Yankees were rolling along through another great season. McCarthy had come into his own as a manager and was leading the Yankees through win after win. He had brought in a new shortstop, Frank Crosetti, and a new third baseman, Joe Sewell. These men helped the defense improve and balanced out the still-amazing hitting. The Yankees once again became a team to fear.

As always, Lou and Babe had a lot to do with the team's success. On June 3, 1932, Lou set a Yankee record that still stands.

The Yankees were playing the Philadelphia Athletics at Shibe Park in Philly. It was just another ordinary day at the stadium until Lou hit his second, then third, then *fourth* home run. No one had hit four home runs in a single game in the twentieth century. No one on the Yankees has done it since. Lou even had a chance to add to his tally when in the ninth inning he slammed a ball straight out to center field. Everyone thought it was gone, but Philadelphia's Al Simmons ran his heart out to catch the ball before it could make it over the wall.

On the day Lou hit four home runs in one game, he also became the first player to hit *three* home runs in four games.

The Yankees were back on top in 1932, beating the Athletics to the pennant by thirteen games. They faced the Chicago Cubs in the World Series, and it was anything but a sportsmanlike atmosphere. The Yankees took the first two games at Yankee Stadium, 12–6 and 5–2. Lou recorded one home run in the first game and had three hits in the second.

The team then traveled to Chicago's Wrigley Field, where they were met by boos, jeers, and even spitting from the Cubs' fans. The Cubs players joined in on the immaturity, shouting insults at Babe Ruth whenever he came to the plate. Meanwhile the Yankees learned that the Cubs were being unfair to a new member of the team—former Yankee Mark Koenig. Although Koenig had been instrumental in getting the Cubs to the series, the team voted to give him only a half share of their World Series money. Supporting their former teammate, the Yankees shouted insults back at the Cubs' dugout, saying they were stupid and moneygrubbing.

Ruth shut everyone up in the fifth inning when he hit a home run that has become a legend. The game was tied 4–4 when Babe came to the plate. The count was two balls and two strikes. Babe pointed into the distance. Some people say he was telling everyone he was going to hit the next pitch into the stands. Others say he was pointing at the pitcher or the Cubs' dugout to irritate them while they shouted at him. Whatever the case, Babe did slam the next ball over center field—the longest home run ever hit at Wrigley Field.

As Babe crossed home plate, Lou was there to congratulate him as always. Babe laughed and told Lou to do the same thing. So Lou did. He was almost hit by the first pitch and had to fall to the ground to escape the ball, but he hammered the second pitch right out of the park. It was his second home run of the game. The Yankees went on to win 7–5.

The Yankees entered the fourth game hoping for their third

World Series sweep. What would stick it to the Cubs and their loudmouthed fans better than shutting them out? But after the first inning the Yankees were behind 4–1. It didn't look good. The Yankees came back, however, and tied the game 5–5, where the score stayed for six innings. A new hero emerged, however—not Lou or Babe, but Tony Lazzeri, who hit two two-run homers in the late innings. The Yankees won the game 13–6 and swept the series, sending their rivals home without much to shout about.

> 66 *Let's face it. I'm not a headline guy. I always knew that as long as I was following Babe to the plate I could have gone up there and stood on my head. No one would have noticed the difference. When the Babe was through swinging, whether he hit one or fanned, nobody paid any attention to the next hitter. They all were talking about what the Babe had done.* 99
>
> —LOU GEHRIG

Lou was the undisputed hitting champion of the series. He had a .529 average, hit three home runs, scored nine runs, and had eight RBIs. Babe had only a .333 average, but it's his called shot that people remember about this series. Babe Ruth's theatrics went down in history, even though Lou had done at least as much to help the team become that year's champions.

Lou may have come home a winner, but he was faced with a war when he arrived at his parents' house. Eleanor couldn't take living with the constant insults of Lou's mother anymore. At one point, she had even broken off the engagement, but Lou won her back within a few hours. It was decided, however, that Eleanor would move in with her aunt and uncle on New York's Long Island until the wedding, which was planned for September 29, 1933—the last day of the regular season. Lou and Eleanor didn't want to try to squeeze their wedding and honeymoon into Lou's baseball schedule.

So Lou had to get through a whole baseball season before marrying the love of his life. On August 17, in a game against the St. Louis Browns, Lou played in his 1,308th game, breaking the record for the longest consecutive-games-played streak. The previous record had been held by Everett Scott, the former Yankees shortstop. Lou was presented with a silver trophy for his accomplishment. It was an honor, but Lou was more focused on the fact that his hitting seemed to be in a slump. He hadn't hit a home run in weeks. Ever the team player, it was more important to him to help the team to win games than it was to be recognized for simply doing his job. Lou finally hit two home runs on August 20 to break the drought, but his end-of-season numbers weren't great by Gehrig standards. He hit .334, scored thirty-two home runs, and had 139 RBIs. To make matters worse, the Yankees, with a great record of ninety-one wins and fifty-nine losses, still came in second in the pennant race. The Washington Senators went to the World Series, and the Yankees went home.

Lou played in his first All-Star game in 1933 and returned every year to represent the AL at first base through 1938.

Amid all these ups and downs, Lou and Eleanor had purchased an apartment in New Rochelle, New York, only a few blocks from Lou's parents' house. They were planning a big wedding celebration for the night of Friday, September 29, and things were going according to plan. Then, the night before the wedding was to take place, Lou got into a huge fight with his mother. She told him she wasn't coming to the wedding because she didn't approve of Eleanor.

Lou had finally had enough. His mother had sworn she would never attend the wedding, but Lou was worried that she might instead show up and ruin the whole event. To avoid such a spectacle, he and Eleanor decided to just get it over with on their own terms. On the morning of September 29, Eleanor was still readying their new apartment. She was with her mom, her aunt, and a bunch of plumbers and carpet layers when Lou called his good friend Walter Otto, the mayor of New Rochelle. The mayor came over and married Eleanor and Lou right there in the middle of their living room with workers walking in and out, Eleanor in an apron, and Lou in a shirt with rolled-up sleeves.

Right after the ceremony, Lou and Eleanor took off for the stadium, accompanied by a fleet of cops on motorcycles. (The mayor had ordered them to escort Lou and his new bride.) Lou failed to get a hit against the Washington Senators in this last game of the season, but he played a perfect game in the field. The Yankees lost, but for once Lou wasn't so upset. After the game, the newlywed ballplayer posed for the press with his wife.

In the off-season, Lou decided that he had to put an end to his mother's attacks on Eleanor once and for all. He realized that his mother wasn't so upset about his wife but was worried about her own financial future now that Lou had someone else to support. So Lou put all of his savings in trust for his parents, bought his mother a new car, and gave her the deed to her house. She was much more agreeable after that.

Chapter Eight

Captain Lou

Although Lou thrived during the 1934 baseball season, his friendship with Babe Ruth started to suffer. The press speculated about the obvious coldness that had developed between the two players. Some said that Lou had finally had enough of being in Babe's shadow. While Lou's lesser star status may have contributed to the bad feelings, that wasn't why the stalemate started.

According to Eleanor Gehrig, the whole thing began as an argument between Mom Gehrig and Babe's second wife, Claire. Babe had adopted a daughter, Dorothy, with his first wife, who had died in a fire. At one point, Babe and Claire went away on a vacation, leaving teenage Dorothy with the maid at home. Dorothy took it upon herself to visit Mom Gehrig, with whom she and her parents had often had dinner. Mom Gehrig decided Dorothy was being neglected by her parents, and she said as much to Babe and Claire after they picked up Dorothy from the

Gehrigs' house. Claire resented Mom Gehrig for interfering, and the argument between the Ruths and the Gehrigs began. By the time spring training began in 1934, the misunderstanding had blown up into a real rift. Babe and Lou weren't talking.

But the argument didn't affect Lou's performance. The 1934 season was his best yet. While Babe Ruth started to decline—he was thirty-nine years old, out of shape, and past his baseball prime—Lou emerged as a true star. He won baseball's Triple Crown that year, with a league-high forty-nine home runs, 165 RBIs, and a .363 batting average.

In the middle of the 1934 season, Lou came close to breaking his games-played streak when he got a bad cold and an ache in his back. In a game in Detroit against the Tigers, he was in so much pain that he was only able to come in for one hit, then spent the rest of the game resting.

The rule preventing former MVP winners from winning again was changed in 1930. But even so, Lou wasn't voted the league MVP. The honor went to Detroit's Mickey Cochrane, who had led his team to the pennant, beating the Yankees, who ended up in second place. Their season over, both Lou and Babe were invited to join an All-Star tour that would take them to Japan to play in exhibition games. Even though they were still fighting, neither man could pass up such an opportunity. So they joined a bunch of their friends, teammates, and rivals from across the league on the trip. They departed by ship from Vancouver, Canada, in October 1934, neither man acknowledging the other as they boarded.

---

66 *They didn't get along. Lou [Gehrig] thought [Babe] Ruth was a big-mouth and Ruth thought Gehrig was cheap. They were both right.* 99

—Yankee teammate Tony Lazzeri

On the crossing from Canada to Japan, another incident only widened the breach between Lou and Babe. Eleanor Gehrig and Claire Ruth, who had been ignoring each other just as their husbands had been, ended up talking on the deck. They found out that they both thought the argument was silly, and Claire invited Eleanor back to her cabin for a snack. Eleanor spent the next couple of hours hanging out with Babe and his wife, feeling like she was making some kind of progress in bringing the two families back together.

Little did she know, at the same time, Lou was getting more and more worried about his wife. He walked the ship, searching for her, and even had a bunch of the ship's crew helping out. After two hours, Lou was sure his wife had fallen overboard, and he was in a panic. He was ready to blast the boat's distress signal and send everyone looking over the side for a body.

Lou was relieved when Eleanor came up from below safe and sound, but he was also angry that she'd made him worry. When he found out she'd been with the Ruths, he uncharacteristically lost his temper, saying it was all Babe's fault. Eleanor tried to explain, and Babe even offered Lou a hug to end the stalemate, but Lou was too upset. He turned his back on Babe once again.

The tour finally arrived in Japan, and Lou was shocked at the number of fans that greeted them. Who knew that people in such a faraway land would care anything about American ballplayers? During the Yankees' first exhibition game against a Japanese team, the fans in the stands gasped each time a player hit a home run. Unlike American fans, the Japanese people didn't crowd the team right after the game. Instead they waited in the halls at the hotel, and, when Lou woke up in the morning, they greeted him with small gifts and thank-yous.

Lou and the All-Star team took their stellar baseball show to various cities in Japan, wowing the crowd each time. Once the team's tour was over, Lou and Eleanor decided to take the honeymoon they never had. They ended up on a world tour, traveling to places like Singapore, India, and Egypt, as well as Italy, Germany, and other parts of Europe. They made Paris, France, the last stop before heading back to the United States and Lou's baseball contract negotiations.

❝*I always wondered every year whether the Yanks would sign me again.***❞**

—LOU GEHRIG

In the past, Lou had always signed his contract and sent it right back for fear that the Yankees might change their mind about him. But he'd been working hard and performing well for the Yankees for a long time. In 1935 he decided to take a stand. He wanted $40,000, and Colonel Jacob Ruppert, the owner of the Yankees, was offering only $39,000. With a difference of only $1,000, it was obviously a symbolic holdout. Lou just wanted to feel appreciated.

Ruppert wouldn't give in, and Lou ended up missing all of spring training. But as the regular season approached, Lou couldn't imagine not being there to take the field with his team. He gave in and settled on $39,000—the highest salary of his career.

In late May, Babe, who had been showing his age, decided to leave the Yanks. Ruth thought Joe McCarthy was a bad manager and wanted Colonel Ruppert to replace McCarthy with

Ruth himself! Ruppert thought the idea of putting the most undisciplined player he'd ever had in charge of the team was ridiculous. Once Babe realized he was never going to manage the Yankees, he left the team in a huff and went to play for and assist with managing the Boston Braves.

Lou must have been relieved to see Babe Ruth go. There would be no more awkward silences, no more avoiding him in the clubhouse. Plus with Ruth gone, no one overshadowed Lou's achievements. For a long time, Lou had been the symbolic leader of the Yankees, and in May, Joe McCarthy offered him the official captainship. Lou was honored to have the title.

> Lou and his wife made a pact that he would retire when he hit age thirty-five, before he started to slow down.

The 1935 season wasn't a great one for either Lou or his team. Lou had only 119 RBIs, which was a team high but a rather low number for him. He had thirty home runs and 176 hits, both big drops from the year before. The Yankees finished the season with a record of 89 wins and 60 losses, putting them in second place in the pennant race for the third year in a row. This time they lost the pennant to the Detroit Tigers. Even though Joe McCarthy didn't have any complaints about Lou's performance, he knew that he had to make a change. When Babe left, he had taken that one-two Ruth-Gehrig punch with him, and the team had suffered. George Selkirk, Babe's replacement in right field, pulled off a respectable .312 batting average, but he had only eleven home runs. The Yankees needed a new hitting partner for Lou if they wanted to get back to the World Series.

Chapter | Nine

A New Partner

Before the 1936 season began, the Yankee management decided that they needed to find a power hitter, someone to complement Lou Gehrig the way Babe Ruth had. They wanted that good old one-two punch back. Joe DiMaggio had been making headlines in the Pacific Coast League for four years. He was a phenomenal hitter with a batting average close to .400. He was exactly what the Yankees needed.

Babe Ruth retired in 1935 after one horrible season with the Boston Braves. The team never gave him a chance to manage as they had promised, so he argued with owner Emil Fuchs and walked out at the end of the season.

Unfortunately for Lou, the moment the New York press got wind of the fact that Joe was coming to the Yanks, they could talk about nothing else. Joe was already a huge star, and he took Babe's place in more than one way. He overshadowed Lou in the press and with the fans from the second he walked into spring training. While Lou was still quiet, reserved, and humble, Joe had a certain confidence and star power that drew people to him.

If Lou cared about being pushed from the spotlight yet again, he didn't show it. Ever the sportsman and gentleman, he was just happy to see the Yankees start winning again.

❝Joe became the team's biggest star almost from the moment he hit the Yanks. It just seemed a terrible shame for Lou. He didn't seem to care, but maybe he did.**❞**

—YANKEE PITCHER LEFTY GOMEZ

During the 1936 season, the Yankees averaged seven runs a game. They clinched the AL pennant by September 9, the earliest clinch in AL history. They were nineteen and a half games ahead of the second-place team, the Detroit Tigers. But it wasn't just the team that was racking up big numbers. Lou had his share of records as well. He hit fourteen home runs against one team—the Cleveland Indians—which was a major league record for homers against a single team. He was also back on top of the home run heap with forty-nine, and this time he didn't have to share the title with anyone else. Lou batted .354 and had 152 RBIs. This was his eleventh straight year with more than a hundred runs batted in. It all added up to Lou's second MVP award. He was back on top of his game.

By contrast, Joe DiMaggio—the team's supposed star—had just twenty-nine home runs, 125 RBIs, and an average of .323. These were all great numbers but not even close to Lou's.

It wasn't just the award and the stats that made this season memorable for Lou. During the World Series, he hit a homer that he said was his biggest thrill in baseball. The series was played against the New York Giants, the Yankees' old hometown rivals. One of the Giants' pitchers, Carl Hubbell, had made a lot of predictions that the Yankees wouldn't be able to get a hit off him. Back in the 1934 All-Star game, Hubbell's screwball had left Lou and a bunch of other hitters dazed. Hubbell was certain he could do it again. Before the series began, the press made a big deal of the matchup. The editors of *Time* magazine even put Gehrig and Hubbell on the cover.

Lou disliked cocky, loudmouthed players more than anything, and he went into the series hoping to put Hubbell in his place with a good hit. Hubbell pitched the first game at the Giants' stadium—the Polo Grounds. Unfortunately, it seemed that the Giants' pitcher had been right to brag. Try as he might, Lou failed to get a hit in four at bats, and the Yankees lost 6–1.

Whenever the Yankees lost, Lou was quiet for the entire car ride back to his home in New Rochelle. He never got used to losing.

The second game was a different story, although Hubbell wasn't pitching that day. Lou hit two singles, knocking in three runs, and the Yankees won 18–4. Then the series moved to Yankee Stadium, where a pitching battle broke out, keeping the score down to 2–1. The Yankees won, thanks in part to a home run hit by Lou in the second inning—his fiftieth of the year.

Lou always remembered the fourth game of the series. Carl Hubbell was pitching again, giving Lou a second chance to show him up. Lou had never hit a ball out of the infield against Hubbell. Meanwhile Hubbell had racked up seventeen wins in a row—a staggering number—and no one had hit a home run against him all year when another player was on base.

It seemed as if the crowd was holding their breath as the two men faced off. Just to make it even more dramatic, Lou and Hubbell battled up to a 3–2 count. Lou didn't want to walk, however. He wanted to slam a ball right out of the park. Even though the next pitch was high and inside, Lou swung at it hard. The ball jetted into the right-field bleachers. The crowd went crazy. Lou had hit a two-run homer against his rival.

"I've had thrills galore. But I don't think any of them top that one," Lou said later. The Yanks went on to win the game 5–2, with Lou hitting a double in later innings.

❝I feel safe in saying that if it weren't for Babe Ruth, Gehrig would have been the great home run hitter of his time.**❞**

—FORMER YANKEE WHITEY FORD

In the fifth game, the Yanks went down 5–4 in the tenth inning after battling hard all day. After his triumphant fourth game, the fifth was a wash for Lou. He had a single but was also thrown out at home when he hesitated for a second too long after Dickey hit a grounder. Had Lou taken off right away and scored, the Yanks could have pulled out a win. The trip up was soon forgotten, however, as the Yankees went on to win the sixth game and the series with a 13–5 battering of the Giants.

Lou and the Yankees ended the 1936 season in triumph, but Lou was about to be dealt a blow from an unlikely source.

In the early months of 1937, Babe Ruth, who was retired and out of the public eye, started to talk to the press about Lou. Unfortunately, he had nothing good to say. Apparently jealous of the fact that Lou could still play and could still make the headlines, Babe gave an interview stating that Lou's consecutive-games-played streak was only going to force him to retire early—that he was going to wear himself out.

"This Iron Man stuff is just baloney," Babe said. "I think he's making one of the worst mistakes a ballplayer can make." He also said the streak statistic was boring, apparently comparing it to his own "exciting" record of sixty home runs in a season.

Lou was upset by the unprovoked interview and made a public statement of his own. "I don't see why anyone should belittle my record or attack it. I never belittled anyone else's," Lou said. The two men didn't play together anymore, hardly ever saw each other, but they still had a tough relationship.

Even though Lou was getting older, he was still at the top of his game. He was rapidly approaching thirty-five, the age at which he'd promised his wife he would retire. The question was, what would Lou do after his baseball career was over?

Publicist Christy Walsh had an answer. Why not get into film? Lou was a handsome and athletic guy. Walsh thought he'd be a natural to make it in Hollywood. Lou wasn't sure that being in front of the camera was the best idea. He wasn't a showman.

But he decided it was worth a try, and that winter he went to Hollywood, California, for a screen test. He ended up signing a one-picture deal with Principal Productions for a film to be made later, after the 1937 season was over.

Lou then focused on the upcoming baseball season, which turned out to be a dazzler! DiMaggio improved on his solid first-year numbers, hitting forty-six home runs, recording 167 RBIs, and earning a .346 batting average. This time he beat out Lou, who finished with thirty-seven homers and 159 RBIs. Lou, how-ever, had a better average at .351. Lou also had 200 hits, meeting or topping the 200 mark for the eighth time in his career. Like when Lou and Babe played together, Lou and Joe seemed to push each other to succeed just by being excellent players themselves.

Lou's favorite moment of the 1937 season came in the All-Star game, when he faced down another impossible pitcher. Jay "Dizzy" Dean of the St. Louis Cardinals would be taking the mound for the National League. He had been quoted as saying that he was "the greatest pitcher in baseball." Once again, Lou was going up against a bragging pitcher and couldn't wait to battle with him.

Before the game, Dean predicted none of the AL players would be able to hit his "fogball." Lou laughed and replied, "I don't know about that. Don't be surprised if I knock one out of the lot off Diz."

Just like in the World Series game against Hubbell, Lou and Dean battled up to a 3–2 count in the third inning. Then Dean threw his fastball, and Lou responded by smacking it into the right-field stands. It was a moment that Lou ranked right up there with the Hubbell homer of '36.

Still, the Yankees had *this year's* series to play. Early in the season, the Yankees had pulled ahead of the Tigers and then never wavered. They finished the 1937 season with 102 wins, thirteen games ahead of the second-place Detroit team. They would face the Giants in the World Series once again. This year even Bill Terry, the Giants' manager, knew his team had no chance. He said that betting on the Giants would be a sucker bet (a bet you can't win). He was right.

The Yankees-Giants rivalry was quickly heating up, and 120,000 fans packed Yankee Stadium for the first two games. They watched the Yankees beat the Giants by a score of 8–1 in both games. Hubbell pitched the first game again, this time giving Lou the respect he deserved by intentionally walking him. Hubbell wasn't going to take a chance on pitching to the guy who had homered off him the year before. As a result, Lou ended the game with no hits.

In the second 8–1 victory, Lou managed a single and was intentionally walked twice. It was great that the pitchers feared him so much, but Lou was disappointed. He wanted to get in the game.

He was finally able to contribute in game three, played at the Polo Grounds. In the fourth inning, Lou hit a double and ended up tying Ruth's record for RBIs in World Series games at thirty-three. The Yankees won 5–1.

In game four, Hubbell was back on the mound and was finally able to scrounge a win for the Giants to avoid the sweep. Lou hit a home run in the ninth and recorded his thirty-fourth World Series RBI, inching ahead of Babe. It wasn't enough to help his team to a win, however, as the Yankees went down 7–3.

They weren't down for long, however. The fifth game was tied 2–2 in the fifth inning when Lou came up with a double that drove in a run and broke the tie. The Yankees went on to win the game 4–2 and took the series from the Giants for the second year in a row.

That fall Lou traveled to California to make his acting debut in the movie *Rawhide* while Eleanor stayed in New York. While Lou was in Hollywood, he went to all the studio parties and events that Christy Walsh told him to go to. The parties were good photo opportunities and would help Lou publicize his new career. The one thing Lou wouldn't do, however, was pose with starlets and showgirls. He had too much respect for Eleanor to be pictured with other women.

The movie premiered in St. Petersburg, Florida, in March 1938, while the Yankees were there for spring training. The town turned the premiere into a carnival with a parade and fireworks. In the film, Lou played himself—on a horse. He traveled to the Wild West, where he stumbled on a town that was being terrorized by bandits. Lou helped the townspeople defeat the bad guys before returning to spring training.

 In one scene in *Rawhide,* Lou knocks out the bad guys by throwing billiard balls at their heads.

Lou did a fair acting job in a bad movie, but it was clear that his first instincts were right—he didn't belong in front of a camera. Lou Gehrig belonged at first base and at the plate, and he was more than happy to get back there.

Chapter | Ten

The Streak and the Slump

When Lou reported for spring training in 1938, he was a few pounds overweight. Lou loved to eat, and his habits were catching up to him. The weight wasn't enough to be alarmed about, but Lou was disappointed in himself. He trained extra hard in the month before the season started and even ran laps in a rubber shirt to sweat the weight off. His strategy worked, and he returned to Yankee Stadium in top form.

On May 30, 1938, the night before Lou's historic streak would hit the 2,000-game mark, his wife urged him to skip the next day's game. Lou and all the people around him had become obsessed with the streak, and reaching 2,000 was the focus. Eleanor knew it was going to be a big story but joked that it would make an even bigger story if Lou just stopped at 1,999 for no apparent reason. She knew, however, that Lou was never going to miss a game unless he was sicker than a dog. He wouldn't do that to his fans and teammates. So on May 31, 1938, Lou played in his 2,000th game against the Boston Red Sox in Yankee Stadium.

❝I had him for over eight years and he never gave me a moment's trouble. I guess you might say he was kind of my favorite.❞

—YANKEES MANAGER JOE McCARTHY

The Yankees gave Lou a horseshoe of flowers to mark the occasion—the same kind of flower arrangement given to a jockey after a big win. A lot of athletes would have spent the night on the town, celebrating with teammates, friends, and the press. But Lou was a family man. He and Eleanor celebrated alone in their apartment with a bottle of champagne.

Soon after that great mark of 2,000 games was reached, however, it became clear that Lou was slowing down. While the Yankees were rolling along with win after win, Lou wasn't contributing the way he used to. At one point in the season, his batting average dropped to a dismal .277. He had a bit of a rally in August, bringing it up to .295, but it was the first time in twelve years that he'd finished below .300. He had only twenty-nine home runs and 114 RBIs.

The press figured Lou was just slowing down due to his age and the staggering number of games he'd played in. Lou, however, couldn't write it off so easily. He put the same power into his swing, so he couldn't understand why the balls weren't flying so hard and fast. He and Joe McCarthy tried to come up with reasons for the slump. Lou changed his batting stance and tried a lighter bat, but when that didn't help, he went back to his old ways. It wasn't until he returned to his original stance and bat weight toward the end of the season that he slightly improved.

And it wasn't just Lou's hitting that was suffering. His reflexes at first base were slow and so was his baserunning. This had to be more than a regular slump. On September 27, Lou hit his last home run of the season at Yankee Stadium against Washington.

❝I tired in midseason. I don't know why, but I just couldn't get going again.**❞**

—LOU GEHRIG ON THE 1938 SLUMP

Even with Lou's drop in production, the Yankees still managed to make the World Series, driven by the power of DiMaggio, George Selkirk, Bill Dickey, and the stellar pitching squad. They would face the Chicago Cubs.

The opening game took place in Chicago, where the Yankees won 3–1. Lou walked once, struck out twice, and hit a single. In the second game, Lou again had only one hit—another single, as the Yankees beat the Cubs 6–3. For the third game, the series moved to Yankee Stadium, where Lou hit another single and scored one run. The Yankees won the game 5–2.

Up three games to none, the Yankees were on the verge of making history. This could be their fourth sweep in six series, and they could become the first team ever to win three straight World Series. In the eighth inning, Lou hit another single. The Yankees took the game by a score of 8–3.

Lou, of course, was disappointed by his series performance, but it was the team's win that mattered most. He knew that the Yankees had made history and that he had played a part in it. The press, however, wanted to know if Lou thought he was done. Had this season been the first in a downward spiral? They asked Lou if he had concerns about 1939. "None at all. Why should I? I just had a bad year last year," Lou responded.

But both Lou and Eleanor knew there was something physically wrong with the Iron Horse. In the off-season, Lou went to a doctor who diagnosed him with a gallbladder problem. The doctor told Lou that if he ate a bland diet, his health would improve. It soon became clear that the problem was worse than the doctor thought. Lou stumbled on his skates when he and

Eleanor went to the ice rink that winter. He could barely hold a glass. He walked more slowly and responded more slowly. Lou tried to keep up a brave face, but inside he was worried. He had no idea what was happening.

After agreeing to his first-ever pay cut (a reduction of $3,000) because of the decline in his performance the season before, Lou returned to St. Petersburg for spring training. It was obvious to everyone that something was seriously wrong. He could hardly run the bases, let alone field the ball. He shuffled his feet when he walked and once fell over in the clubhouse trying to pull on his pants. Lou kept working hard, forcing himself through extra practices and running on his own, but nothing helped.

Joe McCarthy was reluctant to give up on Lou, who over the years had become his favorite player and a good friend. When the season began, Lou was still the starting first baseman, but he didn't last for long. Lou played in the first eight games and was unproductive. He had only four singles, one RBI, and no home runs.

Lou Gehrig holds the following all-time Yankee records: most hits (2,721), most RBIs (1,995), most doubles (534), and most triples (163).

After that eighth game, Lou overheard someone in the locker room say, "Why doesn't he quit? He's through. We can't win with him in here." Lou was heartbroken, but he also realized it was true. He was hurting, not helping, his team. That was the last thing in the world a competitor like Lou Gehrig wanted to do.

On May 2, while the team was on a road trip to Detroit, Lou told McCarthy he was done. He wanted the manager to take him out. "It's for the good of the team, Joe. The time has come for me to quit," Lou said.

That afternoon Ellsworth "Babe" Dahlgren started at first base for the Yankees. Everyone in the stands was stunned when they heard about the substitution. Lou's games-played streak was over, at 2,130.

Cal Ripken Jr. was the first and so far the only player to top Lou's consecutive-game streak of 2,130. Ripken beat Lou's record in 1995 and went on to have a streak of his own that ended at 2,632 consecutive games.

After the decision had been made to quit playing, it was time for Lou to find out what was really wrong with him. In June, at the suggestion of a friend, Eleanor called the famous

Mayo Clinic in Rochester, Minnesota, to set up an appointment for Lou. Dr. Harold Habein said he knew what Lou had the moment he saw the way the ballplayer shuffled into the clinic. Habein's mother had died of amyotrophic lateral sclerosis (ALS), and he recognized the symptoms. Still, the clinic put Lou through days of tests before diagnosing him with the disease.

Eleanor, who had always been the head of her little household, made a deal with the doctors not to tell Lou how serious the disease was. She didn't want him to waste the rest of his life feeling sorry for himself and dreading what was to come. The doctors agreed to stay positive with Lou but told Eleanor the truth. Her husband had, at most, two and a half years to live. She heard this news on June 19, 1939—Lou's thirty-sixth birthday.

❝*I would not have traded two minutes of the joy and the grief with that man for two decades of anything with another.*❞

—ELEANOR GEHRIG

Lou was told that he was stuck with the disease and that there was very little they could do to fight it. Eleanor and the doctors broke the news to Lou that he would never play baseball again. Baseball had always been Lou's life, so he took the news hard. But he and Eleanor had decided he would retire at the age of thirty-five anyway, and he was a year older than that. Maybe this was fate's way of forcing him to keep the promise.

The doctors decided to start Lou on an experimental treatment of vitamin E injections. Lou returned to New York to break the news to his coaches and his team. He officially retired from baseball on July 4, 1939, the day he made his famous farewell speech.

Epilogue

The Pride of the Yankees

L ou traveled with the Yankees for the rest of the 1939 season. He fulfilled his captain's duty, walking the lineup card out to the umpire before each game. The players loved having him around because he was always an inspiration. But it was also hard for them to see their old friend and teammate slowing down so much. At the end of the season, Lou moved on from baseball for good.

New York City mayor Fiorello La Guardia offered Lou a job as a parole commissioner for the city of New York. Lou wasn't sure he was qualified for the position. What did he know about government? But when he learned that the job involved helping wayward kids get back on track, Lou couldn't pass it up. He hoped that he could be a good role model, and he took his work of advising parolees very seriously.

In December 1939 Lou received baseball's highest honor

when he was voted into the National Baseball Hall of Fame. Most players have to wait a year after their retirement to become eligible for the hall, but the Baseball Writers' Association waved that rule in Lou's case. They knew he otherwise might not live to see it happen. He was voted in unanimously.

Meanwhile Eleanor moved the household into the Riverdale section of the Bronx. It made travel into the city easier for Lou, and it was a lot closer to the stadium. Lou still made the occasional visit to his old ballpark and was always mobbed by friends. Eleanor also turned their new home into a constant party. She invited over friends who were musicians, singers, actors, and comedians so someone was always there to cheer up and entertain Lou. She made sure that the last years of his life were as comfortable and as happy as they could be.

By late 1940, Lou was confined to the house, but he could still sit in a chair and interact with his wife, parents, and friends. He appreciated everything Eleanor did for him. He knew how strong she was being for him, always keeping up a happy face. Eventually Lou had to take to his bed as his muscles stopped working altogether. The disease progressed quickly, and Lou passed away on June 2, 1941, just seventeen days before his thirty-eighth birthday.

Telegrams poured in from all over the country from players, community members, and kids whose lives Lou had touched. The sportswriters who once ignored Lou's talents wrote all about his virtues and his dominance. Two years after his death, Hollywood released *The Pride of the Yankees,* a film about Lou's life that was nominated for eleven Academy Awards. In it, many of Lou's former teammates played themselves, including Babe Ruth.

Although Lou Gehrig suffered greatly in his last years, his suffering came to have meaning. Before Lou was stricken with ALS, not many people knew about the disease. Even the medical community hadn't studied it much. In the past, people stricken with the disease were often put in homes for the mentally ill and forgotten.

Lou's fight with ALS brought the disease into the public spotlight. There was a new outcry for research. People saw what the illness could do to a strong man like Lou Gehrig and realized it was a serious disease. Since that time, ALS has often been called Lou Gehrig's disease. His battle with this sickness generated significant research that has given doctors and families a much better understanding of the illness.

On June 19, 2003, in honor of what would have been Lou's one-hundredth birthday, the Yankees held a special ceremony before their game against the Tampa Bay Devil Rays. The ceremony was attended by New York City mayor Michael Bloomberg, Helen Hunter (founder of the ALS Association), and Teresa Wright, the actress who played Eleanor Gehrig in *The*

Pride of the Yankees. The team presented the ALS Association with a check to help with research. That same month, the Philadelphia Phillies, who had adopted ALS as their primary charity, held an auction in Lou's name that raised $502,411 for research. The ALS Association celebrated the anniversary with a new fund-raising drive in the hope of finding a cure. Their motto is "Stop the disease that stopped Lou Gehrig."

Lou Gehrig's legacy isn't just about baseball. It's about caring, strength, and endurance—three qualities that could all be used to describe Lou Gehrig himself.

PERSONAL STATISTICS

Name:

Lou Gehrig

Nicknames:

The Iron Horse, Larrupin' Lou

Born:

June 19, 1903

Died:

June 2, 1941

Height:

6'

Weight:

200 lbs.

Batted:

Left

Threw:

Left

BATTING STATISTICS

Year	Team	Avg	G	AB	Runs	Hits	2B	3B	HR	RBI	SB
1923	NYY	.423	13	26	6	11	4	1	1	9	0
1924	NYY	.500	10	12	2	6	1	0	0	5	0
1925	NYY	.295	126	437	73	129	23	10	20	68	6
1926	NYY	.313	155	572	135	179	47	20	16	112	6
1927	NYY	.373	155	584	149	218	52	18	47	175	10
1928	NYY	.374	154	562	139	210	47	13	27	142	4
1929	NYY	.300	154	553	127	166	32	10	35	126	4
1930	NYY	.379	154	581	143	220	42	17	41	174	12
1931	NYY	.341	155	619	163	211	31	15	46	184	17
1932	NYY	.349	156	596	138	208	42	9	34	151	4
1933	NYY	.334	152	593	138	198	41	12	32	139	9
1934	NYY	.363	154	579	128	210	40	6	49	165	9
1935	NYY	.329	149	535	125	176	26	10	30	119	8
1936	NYY	.354	155	579	167	205	37	7	49	152	3
1937	NYY	.351	157	569	138	200	37	9	37	159	4
1938	NYY	.295	157	576	115	170	32	6	29	114	6
1939	NYY	.143	8	28	2	4	0	0	0	1	0
	Totals	.340	2,164	8,001	1,888	2,721	534	163	493	1,995	102

Key: **Avg**: batting average; **G**: games; **AB**: at bats; **2B**: doubles; **3B**: triples; **HR**: home runs; **RBI**: runs batted in; **SB**: stolen bases

FIELDING STATISTICS

Year	Team	Pos	G	C	PO	A	E	DP	FLD%
1923	NYY	1B	9	60	53	3	4	4	.933
1924	NYY	1B	2	10	9	1	0	0	1.000
		OF	1	1	1	0	0	0	1.000
1925	NYY	1B	114	1,192	1,126	53	13	72	.989
		OF	6	11	9	0	2	0	.818
1926	NYY	1B	155	1,654	1,566	73	15	87	.991
1927	NYY	1B	155	1,765	1,662	88	15	108	.992
1928	NYY	1B	154	1,585	1,488	79	18	112	.989
1929	NYY	1B	154	1,549	1,458	82	9	135	.994
1930	NYY	1B	153	1,402	1,298	89	15	109	.989
		OF	1	2	2	0	0	0	1.000
1931	NYY	1B	154	1,423	1,352	58	13	120	.991
		OF	1	4	3	0	1	0	.750
1932	NYY	1B	156	1,386	1,293	75	18	101	.987
1933	NYY	1B	152	1,363	1,290	64	9	102	.993
1934	NYY	1B	153	1,372	1,284	80	8	126	.994
		SS	1	0	0	0	0	0	-.—-
1935	NYY	1B	149	1,434	1,337	82	15	96	.990
1936	NYY	1B	155	1,468	1,377	82	9	128	.994
1937	NYY	1B	157	1,460	1,370	74	16	113	.989
1938	NYY	1B	157	1,597	1,483	100	14	157	.991
1939	NYY	1B	8	70	64	4	2	5	.971
	Total		2,147	20,808	19,525	1,087	196	1,575	.991

Key: Pos: position; G: games; C: chances (balls hit to a position); PO: putouts; A: assists; E: errors; DP: double plays; FLD%: fielding percentage

SOURCES

4 Robinson, Ray, *Iron Horse: Lou Gehrig in His Time* (New York: Norton, 1990), 263.

4 Robinson, Ray, and Christopher Jennison, *Pennants & Pinstripes: The New York Yankees 1903–2002* (New York: Viking Studio, 2002), 65.

4–5 "Farewell Speech," *LouGehrig.com,* n.d., <http://www.lougehrig.com/about/speech.htm> (December 10, 2003).

8 "Quotes About Lou Gehrig," *LouGehrig.com,* n.d., <http://www.lougehrig.com/about/quotesabout.htm> (December 10, 2003).

8 Robinson, *Iron Horse,* 32.

19 Gehrig, Eleanor, and Joseph Durso, *My Luke and I* (New York: Crowell, 1976), 40.

19 Robinson, *Iron Horse,* 41.

20 Ibid., 42.

21 Gehrig, *My Luke and I,* 45.

26 Robinson, *Iron Horse,* 52.

27 Gehrig, *My Luke and I,* 70.

27 Ibid., 70–71.

28 "Quotes About Lou Gehrig," *LouGehrig.com,* n.d., <http://www.lougehrig.com/about/quotesabout.htm> (December 10, 2003).

28 Gehrig, *My Luke and I,* 116.

29 Ibid., 117.

29 Robinson, *Iron Horse,* 62.

31 Robinson, *Iron Horse,* 68.

38 "Quotations From & About Lou Gehrig," *baseball-almanac.com,* n.d., <http://baseball-almanac.com/quotes/quogehr.shtml> (December 10, 2003).

40 Robinson, *Iron Horse,* 86.

41 Ibid., 88.

43 Newman, Mark, "Gehrig's shining legacy of courage," *Yankees.com,* June 18, 2003, <http://newyork.yankees.mlb.com/NASApp/mlb/nyy/history/gehrig.jsp > (December 10, 2003).

49 "Quotes By Lou Gehrig," *LouGehrig.com,* n.d., <http://www.lougehrig.com/about/quotesby.htm> (December 10, 2003).

53 Ibid., 154.

57 Robinson, *Pennants & Pinstripes,* 41.

59 Robinson, *Iron Horse,* 151.

62 Gehrig, *My Luke and I,* 140.

62 Ibid., 142.

66 "Quotes By Lou Gehrig," *LouGehrig.com,* n.d., <http://www.lougehrig.com/about/quotesby.htm> (December 10, 2003).

72 "Quotations From & About Lou Gehrig," *baseball-almanac.com,* n.d., <http://baseball-almanac.com/quotes/quogehr.shtml> (December 10, 2003).

74 Robinson, *Iron Horse,* 66.

78 Ibid., 216.

81 Ibid., 222.

81 Ford, Whitey with Phil Pepe, *Few and Chosen: Defining Yankee Greatness Across the Eras,* (Chicago: Triumph Books), 18.

82 Robinson, *Iron Horse,* 224.

82 Ibid.

82 Ibid., 226

88 "Quotations From & About Lou Gehrig," *baseball-almanac.com,* n.d., <http://baseball-almanac.com/quotes/quogehr.shtml> (December 10, 2003).

89 Gehrig, *My Luke and I,* 210.

90 Ibid.

92 Ibid., 212.

92 Robinson, *Pennants & Pinstripes,* 64.

93 Gehrig, *My Luke and I,* 229.

BIBLIOGRAPHY

Curran, William. *Big Sticks: The Batting Revolution of the Twenties.* New York: William and Morrow, 1990.

Ford, Whitey, with Phil Pepe. *Few and Chosen: Defining Yankee Greatness Across the Eras.* Chicago: Triumph Books, 2001.

Gehrig, Eleanor, and Joseph Durso. *My Luke and I.* New York: Crowell, 1976.

Robinson, Ray. *Iron Horse: Lou Gehrig in His Time.* New York: Norton, 1990.

Robinson, Ray, and Christopher Jennison. *Pennants & Pinstripes: The New York Yankees 1903–2002.* New York: Viking Studio, 2002.

WEB SITES

Lou Gehrig: The Official Web Site

www.lougehrig.com

Lots of great pictures, as well as quotes by and about Lou, including the text of his farewell speech and his career statistics.

ALS Association

www.alsa.org

Learn more about Lou Gehrig's disease and the fight to find a cure.

New York Yankees: The Official Site

http://www.yankees.com

The official Yankees site has a ton of history, including articles about Lou.

Baseball Almanac: Lou Gehrig

www.baseball-almanac.com

Search for Lou Gehrig and find some wonderful stories about Lou, as well as poetry and articles published at the time of his retirement.

The YES Network

http://www.yesnetwork.com/announcers/index.cfm?cont_id=184480&page_type=wide

A great homage to Lou by announcer and writer Phil Pepe, who believes Lou was the most underrated player of all time.

INDEX